Ex Africa semper aliquid novi.
There is always something
new out of Africa.

Proverbial, from Pliny
AD 23-79

A press trip in Biafra, 1968, with army escort. From the front, Walter Partington of the *Daily Express*, Bruce Loudon, a stringer for the *Daily Telegraph*, and Frederick Forsyth, then a freelance. The photographer was David Cairns of the *Express*.

Paul Harrison
Robin Palmer

Hilary Shipman
London

First published October 1986 by
Hilary Shipman Limited
19 Framfield Road
Highbury
London N5 1UU

British Library Cataloguing in Publication Data
Harrison, Paul
    News out of Africa: Biafra to Band Aid.
    1. Reporters and reporting—Africa
    I. Title   II. Palmer, Robin
    070.4'3'096   PN5450

ISBN 0-948096-02-0
ISBN 0-948096-03-9 Pbk

Cover design by David Bennett
Data conversion by ImagePlus
Typeset by Infotype Limited
and printed in Oxford
by Information Printing Limited

Contents

for
Joy Harrison
and
Jocelyn and Joanna Palmer

Acknowledgements

The authors and publishers wish to thank Angus McDermid for providing the *Nigerian Observer*, the report of Colonel Ojukwu's press conference and the Markpress bulletins; David Cairns for the three photographs from Biafra; Don Dornan (Father Kevin Doheny); Thames Television (Jonathan Dimbleby, photographed by Mary Crewe); Nigel Watt (saucepan radio); Camerapix (Mohamed Amin); and the Royal Television Society (Mohamed Amin and Michael Buerk). The photographs of Father Mike Doheny and Bob Geldof with Mother Teresa were taken by Paul Harrison.

The authors

Robin Palmer spent many years in Africa, as a lecturer at the Universities of Zambia and Zimbabwe and as Professor of History at the University of Malawi. He has also taught at the Universities of California, Edinburgh and Oxford. He has written and edited a number of books on Africa, including *Land and Racial Domination in Rhodesia* and *The Roots of Rural Poverty in Central and Southern Africa*, and is an editor of the *Journal of Southern African Studies*.

Paul Harrison's films include the award-winning *Aerial Ambassador* about the Goodyear airship. He has had extensive experience of Africa and has been making films there for nine years, often in connection with the missionary and charity work of Fathers Kevin and Mike Doheny. His film production company, Worldvoice, is currently preparing a television series on Africa.

Preface

I went to Ethiopia in June 1984 with Father Mike Doheny, a founder of the Irish volunteer agency Concern, to make a documentary film about the worsening famine there. I knew from friends in Concern that something was seriously wrong and they asked if I could help them with fund raising and publicity by making a film.

What I saw in Ethiopia appalled me. I felt I should do what I could to publicise it. I came back from Ethiopia with my film, but with no money, house or job. I even had to borrow money from a friend to pay for a telecine service at Visnews to copy the film onto videotape. There at Visnews I stumbled into the news machine for the first time, by accident. Just days later, parts of my film were being shown on ITN's *News At Ten* and *Channel 4 News*. Within weeks the footage was seen in 12 countries.

But it was a later film by Mohamed Amin and Michael Buerk that really blew open the story. What kept up the momentum then was Bob Geldof's reaction to the film, his formation of Band Aid and then the organisation of Live Aid and Sport Aid.

At Christmas '84 I went back to film in Ethiopia, where I met Geldof with a score of journalists in tow. The difference between this and my previous trip was dramatic. Addis Ababa's previously quiet airport was buzzing with relief flights. Aircraft from all over the world crawled around the tarmac with their loads of grain and relief supplies. Ethiopia, for the media, had come of age.

Of course this wasn't the first famine story to emerge from Africa. There had been the Biafran famine in 1968-70, and the 1973 famine in Ethiopia. I knew details of each of them, mainly from two good Irish friends, Frs Mike and Kevin Doheny, who between them have been in most famine areas in the world.

I began to wonder how much the media's reporting of Africa had changed in the two decades between Biafra and Band Aid. There had been dramatic technological improvements in between. I was bewildered at how the media hadn't picked up on Ethiopia before. I realised its power once it got into gear and wanted to find out more. There would be a lot of research. I needed to work with someone who was a writer and knew something about Africa's history. I thought of Robin Palmer whom I'd met in Brussels at a meeting of non-government organisations working in Africa. I was with Fr Kevin and we'd shown my film during a lunch break. Out of several hundred people about a dozen bothered to come – Robin was one of them. He's a historian of Africa and has lived there for 15 years.

We've been helped by a lot of people both in the media and in aid and development. We'd like to thank them all for their co-operation.

They include Mohamed Amin, Michael Buerk, Paddy Coulter, Jonathan Dimbleby, Maggie Eales, Frederick Forsyth, Bob Geldof, Peter Gill, Françoise Husson, Michael Leapman, Colin Legum, Angus McDermid, Graham Mytton, Stewart Purvis, Michael Samuelson, Rob Stephenson, Charles Stewart, Lloyd Timberlake, and a range of people in organisations like Visnews, BBC, ITN, Channel 4 News, Thames Television, TV-am, CNN, TF1, Reuters, Agence France Presse and Soviet TV.

It's been a fascinating project. The media machine is huge, and Africa's problems are many and difficult to present sympathetically and objectively in the west. Earlier stereotypes derived from Tarzan films are now giving way to misleading images of a continent full of nothing but helpless victims. If all we do in this book is to dent some of these stereotypes a little, it will have been worthwhile. But we hope we have done more than that.

Paul Harrison
July 1986

1 | Tripping over the News

When Paul Harrison came back from filming the Ethiopian famine in July 1984, he stumbled into the news machine for the first time and was astonished by what he found. He had been working in the documentary film industry and had made a number of previous trips to Africa. But he had never seen such horrific scenes as those he witnessed in Ethiopia.

He wanted to edit the scenes on videotape and hired a telecine – which converts from film to tape – at Visnews, a giant television news agency. Telecine is an expensive operation – the machines are costly and the process highly skilled. While the film is fed through the machine, the operator watches it closely with a joystick in each hand. His task is to make sure that the best possible image actually goes down on tape. If the colours are too blue on the master 16mm, he rides it with his joystick and tweaks in amounts of red and green to bring it back to normal. If it's too dark, he can 'lift' the picture to make it lighter.

It was not long before Harrison found that his film was more than just another task:

> Shortly after we started two or three other guys joined us. They began to ask questions about the film. I told them about the famine that was devastating Ethiopia. What, they asked, was I planning to do with the footage? Who had the rights? Would I be prepared to sell it as news?
>
> Would I? Here I was at the heart of the world's largest television newsgathering organisation, and they were asking me if they could buy the material!

Harrison immediately agreed. News Coverage Manager Brendan Farrow made a telephone call. The BBC was interested. Brendan made another phone call. The telecine was just about completed when he returned to say that they wouldn't be needing the footage after all. They had contacted their man in Nairobi and there would be a crew going into Ethiopia to film the famine on Monday. It was Saturday.

In fact it took not two days but a further three months to make the films by Mohamed Amin of Visnews with commentary by Michael Buerk, screened by BBC News on 23 and 24 October 1984. But on that Saturday in July, Harrison was alerted to the wider potential of his film. He thought there was an outside chance of it being shown on national television news. In the light of the BBC's interest, perhaps ITN might want to pre-empt them. Harrison phoned John Toker of ITN's foreign desk. Toker asked to see the tape on Sunday afternoon:

> John and I viewed the tape together at high speed. Starving black figures whizzed about the screen in a keystone horror comedy. Occasionally he'd throw them into reverse or slow them to normal speed and ask me a question. 'There's a story there', he said. But he'd have to get approval from his boss.

The next day Harrison returned to collect the tape and to be told: 'Sorry, Africa isn't really an easy story to tell, the public feel it's too far from them and a famine isn't really a nice news item.' It was suggested that he try *Channel 4 News*. They were just upstairs:

> By now I was now beginning to feel a bit of a prostitute, hawking famine and death in these corridors of power. But it would have been irresponsible to turn back, for too much was at stake. I'd gone to Ethiopia to find out what was happening and to tell people about it. If we could reach millions through television, many lives might be saved.
>
> I was also beginning to be puzzled by the attitude of the people I'd met. It certainly wasn't obvious how decisions were made about what was, and what was not, considered newsworthy. It all seemed very random.

Later that Monday Harrison met Helen Armitage, then Foreign News Editor of *Channel 4 News*. She wasn't interested. On Wednesday the phone rang. She was interested. The BBC and ITV were launching a famine appeal that day for several African countries. They met again the next morning and the following Monday, 23 July, his report on Ethiopia's famine went out on *Channel 4 News*.

Harrison watched in the studio as the final cut version, of just over four minutes, went out on the air. The news-hardened technicians stopped and watched in total silence, something that, Harrison was told subsequently, was practically unheard of. It was a reaction that was to be echoed some months later at the BBC and NBC when Amin's film was shown.

Later that evening a cutdown version of the film went out on *News At Ten.* 'ITN's telephone lines started buzzing,' says Harrison. 'Gears started to turn. But it wasn't a patch on what happened later'.

What happened later, of course, was the Amin-Buerk film, catalyst for a huge popular movement and continuing expression of concern.

Famine in Africa was not new, though it had rarely sparked such a massive media campaign. But the 1984 Ethiopian famine was by no means the first African famine to be widely exposed to the world. There had been the one in Biafra in 1968-70. There had been another in Ethiopia in 1973. In each of these three cases it had been the determined efforts of people in different branches of the media which had brought them to light.

In Biafra the reports of Frederick Forsyth prepared the ground for the story of famine, first broken by Michael Leapman through the medium of the press. Jonathan Dimbleby's film in Ethiopia in 1973 not only exposed the famine but triggered a revolution. In 1984 it was television again, with Amin and Buerk. And then came Geldof.

These three famines were also linked through the experiences of Irish Holy Ghost missionaries Mike and Kevin Doheny, who in their own ways exploited the media in order to help in the relief of suffering.

In this book we move from the experiences of Frederick Forsyth in Biafra, at a time when the press still provided most of our news, to today's world of electronic news gathering and satellites, where Live Aid could be seen simultaneously on 85 per cent of the world's television screens.

We discover how Britain is the hub of international news. We illuminate the changes in attitudes and technology over the past 20 years and the way that news and documentary decisions are made.

We have talked at length to the major participants involved in breaking these famine stories. Their testimonies give this book its authority and give us a rare glimpse of the inner workings of the media machine.

We also examine the irony of why, despite the fact that we can now receive live television pictures from anywhere in the world, there is often less informed foreign coverage today than there was two decades ago when Frederick Forsyth went out to cover a 'small bush war' in West Africa.

2 | The Forsyth Saga: Broadcasting from Biafra 1967–68

In July 1967, when a civil war broke out in Nigeria in West Africa, most people in Europe still got their news from either newspapers or radio. This was particularly the case with foreign stories. In Africa, news agencies like Reuters, Agence France Press and Associated Press had been operating for over a century and the written press and radio journalism were also well established. Television journalism was not; the BBC and ITV, when they covered Africa, relied on sending crews from London – resident foreign correspondents were then still a rarity and did not exist in Africa at all. So although television was no longer in its infancy, it did not at that time enjoy the dominant position it now holds in news and current affairs. In those days it was still a major operation to cover a foreign story for television.

The Nigerian civil war at first went almost unnoticed by the western media whose attention had been focused on the Six-Day War in the Middle East. Nigeria had formerly been considered one of Britain's model colonies – a place which young recruits to the colonial service in Africa gave as one of their first preferences for a posting. With the recent discovery of oil there, it was believed that Nigeria, the largest of Britain's former colonies in Africa, would also emerge as the strongest and most successful. It seemed, at first glance, an unlikely place for a civil war. By the time hostilities ended in January 1970 over a million people had died of starvation. Most of them were children. It was the first famine disaster story from Africa to receive wide and continuing coverage in the west. It was not, of course, to be the last.

As the British colonies in Africa first struggled for, and then gained, their independence one by one in the late 1950s and early 1960s, so the 'Dark Continent' emerged briefly from the media shadows. Violence in places like Kenya, Nyasaland and Northern Rhodesia made the front pages of British newspapers. A succession of constitutional conferences brought the new African political leaders to London regularly. While in Britain, they exploited the media to further their cause and established close relations with sympathetic journalists, like Colin Legum of *The Observer* and Patrick Keatley of *The Guardian*, and with MPs, mostly Labour and Liberal. Men like Kwame Nkrumah, Tom Mboya, Julius Nyerere, Kenneth Kaunda and Hastings Banda became well-known names in Britain. It was a time when many of the 'heavy' and the tabloid papers had their Africa or Commonwealth correspondents and when African politics were discussed seriously in both. A dozen Commonwealth correspondents from the serious daily and Sunday papers and the BBC met monthly in the Reform Club to discuss current African problems. A quarter of a century later there is scarcely an Africa correspondent left in Fleet Street.

The journalists and others – economic planners, career diplomats, businessmen and academics – who thought or wrote about Africa in the early 1960s tended to share an optimism which now, with the wisdom of hindsight, appears tragic, misplaced and naïve. It was widely assumed that – with the shackles of colonialism thrown off – Africa was about to enter a new and glorious era. Colin Legum, then Africa and Commonwealth Correspondent of *The Observer*, recalls that anyone who tried to sound a note of caution would be accused of rocking the boat and of unwarranted pessimism. As the African colonies became independent, so their political struggles against the British ended and their leaders came to the west less frequently. It was therefore natural that Africa began to slip out of the public consciousness of the west. The dominant foreign story of the 1960s and beyond became Vietnam, where press and television coverage changed the outcome of the war, for it informed American public opinion in a totally new way and caused many to oppose the war and all that it stood for.

It was against such a background that the Nigerian civil war broke out in 1967. The causes of the conflict were complex. The dominant people of Eastern Nigeria were the Ibos. They were well educated, largely Christian, and entrepreneurs of great renown. Over a period of many years more than a million of them had left their home areas to work in other parts of Nigeria. This became a kind of colonisation. Ibos would take jobs in the predominantly Muslim north as airport controllers, for example, because there was nobody in the north sufficiently qualified. They would then bring up relatives to work in more menial positions as airport porters, canteen staff and the like. This was deeply resented by the northerners, especially by the dominant Hausa, who regarded the Ibos as infidels and segregated them into ghettos. Regional tensions became acute after independence in 1960 as politicians fought ruthlessly for the spoils of office. Civilian politicians soon became thoroughly discredited. In January 1966 there was a bloody Ibo-planned military coup which was followed by a bloodier northern counter-coup in July. In September, Radio Cotonou, in neighbouring Dahomey (now Benin), broadcast a report of some northerners being killed in the east. It wasn't true, but nobody waited to check the story. Northern mobs went on the rampage, brutally killing thousands of Ibo civilians, while Ibo soldiers were hacked to death in army barracks. Those who survived fled to the east, injured, often destitute, and posing massive problems of relocation. Colin Legum wrote moving reports of these terrible events for *The Observer*, comparing them to the great ingathering of Jews into Palestine after the Second World War.

There followed a major exodus of skilled Ibos from other parts of Nigeria, as bus drivers, post office engineers and engine drivers drove their buses, vans and trains to the east. The Nigerian government made little attempt in public to heal the wounds or condemn the atrocities. Easterners, exasperated beyond endurance but comforted too by the presence of oil, felt they had little choice but to break away from Nigeria and establish an independent state – which they called the Republic of Biafra. Civil war followed.

It was widely assumed that this would be a minor bush war, which would be over in days rather than weeks. The Federal Nigerian army was far larger and infinitely better equipped than anything the breakaway easterners could muster. The easterners were thought to be a hopeless rabble of traders, clerks and intellectuals. It didn't look as though it was going to be much of a war – or much of a story, as far as the rest of the world was concerned.

One man who had seen it all coming was Angus McDermid, the BBC's West Africa Correspondent, who was then in the middle of a 12-year stint in various parts of the continent. Stationed in South Africa during the Second World War, McDermid had gone to Nigeria for the first time in 1959, had worked in the Congo and then Rhodesia before taking up his West African post in 1964. He recalls that on the day of the January 1966 coup in Nigeria, Radio

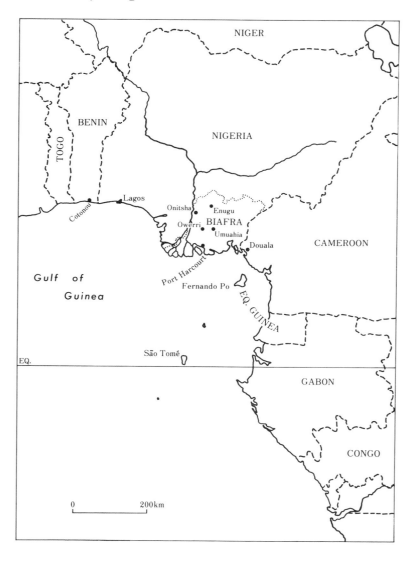

Nigeria, showing Biafra's borders at the time of secession, and other places referred to in the text.

Nigeria opened with an account of a coup – in Indonesia! At the time of the July coup he phoned his wife to tell her the news, speaking in Welsh, before the government censor interrupted: 'You must speak in English or the vernacular.' 'This is my vernacular', McDermid retorted, and continued his conversation. It was a world scoop.

It was quite obvious to McDermid that things were breaking up between Lagos, the Nigerian capital, and the east. He began to cast himself in the role of 'the man for the east', recognising that this was going to be a tough assignment. For some months before the war, he studied the best means of getting news out of what he knew would become a blockaded region. He got a visa for the neighbouring Spanish island of Fernando Po and was 'ready for the off'. As soon as Biafra seceded, he slipped in through the back door from Cameroon, which borders eastern Nigeria. McDermid recalls:

> I got there and set up my communications quite successfully. I was the only outside reporter there at the time; there was nobody else. I was getting stuff out. It did me absolutely no good for one extremely good reason – it was the Six-Day War, so there was nothing about Biafra on the BBC at all, except on the African Service. And there I was, sweating my guts out trying to find stories! I think I got one piece on the air, but the main thing was that the communications were set up.

> Most of the ex-Cable & Wireless communications people were Ibos and they brought all their equipment back from other parts of Nigeria during the great ingathering. They had a telex link with Fernando Po and from there to Lisbon. They had radio links as well. In fact they maintained through the entire period of secession a telex link, thanks to the Portuguese authorities. There were no communications with the rest of Nigeria at all.

> After about five days there, something very strange happened. The Biafrans had a strong transmitter of their own called Radio Biafra, run by ex-Radio Nigeria people. They were very good at radio, as indeed they were on publicity – on communications they were unbeatable. I was intrigued to hear that – according to Radio Biafra – I had been declared *persona non grata* by the Federal authorities. To me it was very significant, because to be West African Correspondent for the BBC without having an

entrée into Nigeria was a distinct handicap!

Radio Biafra said they didn't know where they'd got the story. The obvious thing to do to check up was to go to where I could phone London. So I got out. The Biafrans gave me a Land Rover to the Cross River bridge, and I was the last but one out. Behind me was the Cameroonian Consul who had closed his consulate that day. They ceremoniously closed the gate and that was the last of the road communications that Biafra had with the outside world.

McDermid hitch-hiked down to Douala and there spoke to the BBC in London, who called up Lagos and were told that he had not been declared *persona non grata*. But he decided not to return to Biafra before checking further. He went back to Lagos, saw the Chief Information Officer and asked him if he knew about this:

'No, we didn't know.'
'Well, have I been?'
'No, you haven't.'
'Am I likely to be?'
'Ah, well, you are always welcome in our country, but if you ever set foot in Biafra again, you *will* be declared *persona non grata!*'

So McDermid wondered what to do next. He talked again to the BBC in London, who told him to stay put in Lagos. However, he wasn't satisfied. He replied:

'I think you ought to have somebody in Biafra. A dual situation needs a dual representation. The fun hasn't started yet. Get somebody there quickly.'

And they sent Freddie Forsyth, who was then on the Foreign News staff in London.

Summing up this strange episode, McDermid concludes:

The idea of this false broadcast was that they wanted the status, the kudos, and the lustre that having the BBC West African Correspondent on their side would bring. By this rather childish trick they hoped that I would stay in the east and be their spokesman. This was going to be a great media triumph, but of course it went wrong and I really don't know how they expected me to go along with it.

Back in London, there was little time for a considered decision on who to send out to Biafra. It was the summer holiday season and many correspondents not already on holiday were off covering the aftermath of the Six-Day War. Frederick Forsyth was then a 29-year-old reporter. He had joined the BBC in 1965 after working in Europe for Reuters for four years. Before that he had worked for a local newspaper in Norfolk. The BBC had kept him on domestic work, both radio and television. Forsyth was anxious to work abroad again. He recalls:

> I was sitting alone in an office in London when a head came round the door to ask if I would do them a favour and go out of my normal parish, which was Europe, and go to Africa for what was, they assured me, only a seven-, maybe a ten-day bush war. I had never been to Africa before, apart from a brief visit to Tangier. I didn't particularly want to go. I only went on the understanding that I'd be there for about a couple of weeks at the outside.

This entirely fortuitous assignment to Africa was to change his life. It also paved the way for an African famine story to become a major issue in the west for the first time. When Forsyth helped expose a story which the British government was trying hard to conceal, there was a massive public outcry and a campaign which brought together people of all political persuasions as images of starving African children touched the conscience of the west.

When Forsyth was sent out to cover the Biafran war for the BBC in July 1967, he travelled with Sandy Gall of ITN and a couple of others. Entry to Biafra via the Nigerian capital was now impossible because of the closedown of all communications across the fighting line, so they had to go across the Cameroonian border. Within ten days Forsyth's fellow reporters had filed their stories and left. He found himself alone and in charge of the communications procedures that McDermid had left behind. It took a while for the shooting war to start in earnest. Forsyth remembers his initial briefing, which turned out to be wholly wrong:

> I was told that this was a very small bush uprising led by an ambitious and ruthless colonel [Ojukwu]; the colonel had no support from the Ibo people whatsoever; the whole thing was a storm in a teacup; the Nigerian Army, which was British-trained, was an absolutely magnificent fighting force which would sweep

effortlessly through this rabble of Ibo tribesmen who were
regarded very contemptuously as 'the Jews of Africa', and who
obviously couldn't fight.

I was to make first base with the British Deputy High Commissioner in Enugu, Jim Parker, and he would gather round him
the remaining British community and we would all move
southwards ahead of the oncoming and all-conquering Nigerian
Army towards Port Harcourt, from where we would be
evacuated outwards to Cameroon. When I got there I was to
file a summary of this ten-day war.

It wasn't as simple as that. The war was in fact to last for two-
and-a-half years and the extent of Biafran resistance, aided by a
skilful and judicious propaganda campaign, was to surprise friend
and foe alike. Forsyth clearly relished his new challenge. Angus
McDermid recollects:

You had a very heady atmosphere of revolt. Biafra was fighting
for its existence. This was a very romantic situation, and really
nothing like it had occurred in African politics before. It was
an excellent news story. Freddie reported very fully and very
enthusiastically. I went back to London – we worked three
months on and three months off – and I remember hearing some
of his despatches. They were very vivid. He was up with the
troops alright. He became reviled by the Federal soldiers; they
called him 'backsight' – a big joke in the Nigerian army!

So the BBC, for what turned out to be a very brief period, began
by covering both sides of the war on radio, with McDermid and
Peter Stewart alternating in Lagos and with Forsyth in Biafra.
There was some tension between the reports coming out of the
two sides, which reflected the greater difficulty of getting access
to any hard news on the Federal side. There was also a certain
amount of television coverage, mostly on current affairs programmes like *Panorama*, but it tended to concentrate on interviews with
political leaders. Bush wars, then as now, are notoriously difficult
to film, though Sandy Gall got some reports onto *News at Ten*.

The Nigerian war was initially a slow war of attrition, unspec-
tacular from a televisual perspective. The technology of the time
didn't help much either, according to Forsyth:

It used to be the case that a crew going to cover an outside event needed close to half a ton of equipment. There were huge Auricon cameras or Arriflexes. They involved big heavy mahogany stands on which they had to be mounted and large battery packs and quite sizeable magazines that had to be changed regularly. Once it had been taken, the cameraman had to go under a hood, remove the film from the camera, put it in a sealed circular tin, identify it and wrap it round with masking tape. All these tins then had to be flown from where the photography had taken place back to a studio in London. There it had to be developed with the old chemical processes, spliced together, run through a Movieola and then the cutting took place. Finally you ended up with a piece of film which you could show on the evening news.

It was a long and slow process. It was long inasmuch as getting the crew out there was lengthy and tiresome because of the amount of gear they had to get through customs, and the amount they had to pay in excess baggage to get these enormous aluminium chests on board the aircraft. Humping the stuff from the hotel, for example, to the battle or revolution or refugee camp – whatever it was you wanted to photograph – was a slow process. So was getting the film flown back and then the whole development process. You were talking of two to three days to hitting the evening news.

Film was used then, not video. And other technology was also far less sophisticated then than it is today. Telex was not widespread and the quality of the international telephone system was so poor that direct phone interviews with foreign correspondents were rare. Newspaper journalists had the edge over radio reporters until the development of the 'link-up' circuit which allowed correspondents to report 'down the line' from foreign broadcasting stations to London. These monologue reports would be taped, edited and included in radio news bulletins. But such communication facilities were not available in Biafra, with its one telex link with the outside world.

Forsyth, as the sole remaining western journalist in Biafra, gradually discovered that the confident predictions made by British officials were way off beam. He reported that in most stand-up fights the Biafrans were giving as good as they got, and that the war was getting bogged down:

Frederick Forsyth with the Biafran leader Colonel Ojukwu at his headquarters in Umuahia.

After two months it was quite clear to me that this wasn't a small bush uprising; that Ojukwu was a massively charismatic figure who enjoyed the support of probably 90 per cent of his people; that their support was fanatical, and that they were fighting tooth and claw. It was also clear to me that the Nigerian Army was a rabble, a shambles from beginning to end and that Gowon was no leader. I formed the view that this was going to be a very long affair and could potentially be extremely bloody. I filed that viewpoint.

This was apparently not good news for the British government, which was hoping for a quick and relatively bloodless Federal victory. According to Forsyth:

It did not amuse the Commonwealth Office. In fact it brought the British High Commissioner in Lagos to transports of irritation. He flew back to London and briefed the CO on the damage that this callow young reporter from the BBC was doing. The CO didn't approach the BBC at Broadcasting House; it went to Bush House, the Overseas Service, where of course it had enormous clout. The Head of West African Services got the message and relayed the objection to Broadcasting House. I was duly summoned back in September.

I got back to an extraordinary reception which took me completely by surprise. In essence, I was summoned to the office of the Foreign News Editor to be told that he and indeed the entire BBC were extremely dissatisfied with the reports that I'd filed, which stunned me. I asked why. I said that I was confident that I could bring four or five witnesses to confirm their validity. This wasn't required at all – a judgement had already been made.

Finally at another interview it was made plain to me, because I pressed for answers, that I had upset the Commonwealth Office. That was obviously the crime. I was told that I would never report another foreign assignment for the BBC. I had upset powerful interests and that was the end of that.

Friends in the BBC found Forsyth temporary posts in London while he contemplated his future. At this stage the Nigerian civil war was still a very localised, low-casualty affair with no heavy weaponry involved. As yet, there were no signs of famine. In

January 1968 the Biafrans invited a large British press corps to go down on a facility trip to see things for themselves. The BBC decided not to send anyone. Forsyth went up to Broadcasting House to ask why and was told: 'Our policy is that we are not covering that war', and that the subject was now taboo. Simultaneously he learned that there had been a few covert arms flights out of Gatwick to Nigeria, though this had been roundly denied in Parliament:

> I became so suspicious about what was going on that I actually looked at my leave status and discovered that I had a week owing. So I took it after the group who had gone on the facility trip had come back. The stories that they wrote seemed to me to fulfil just about every forecast I had made and to vindicate all that I had said, which had been pooh-poohed at the time as boyish nonsense or blatant lies, whichever view you took of my reports. So I took a week's leave and went down off the cuff and off the record, paying my own fare.

> I returned to Britain on the Wednesday, resigned from the BBC on the spot, and flew back to Biafra on the Friday. I was now career-less and I left behind some bemusement, because there were various reports that I had defected to Russia, that I had gone mad, or that I had disappeared into the bush!

The BBC sent out a senior administrator to try to persuade Forsyth to return. He declined. The die was cast. Forsyth was to play a crucial role in publicising the Biafran cause and the famine which exploded all over the world's press in 1968-9. Looking back at this crucial turning point in his career, he reflects that:

> My main motive was anger at the cover-up. I am a reporter to my boot heels and I don't like managed news. I knew there was a conspiracy of silence way back in October 1967. Someone, somewhere, was trying to tell us what we should read, what we should listen to, what we should see, and I didn't like that.

> For me the issue was twofold. There was a brutal and callous cynicism operated by my government, which I am in part responsible for, towards a people who had done us no harm, never threatened our assets or the security of our nation. Yet it had been decided to sentence them to death by some process in an office in London. That, I thought, was wrong. It wasn't that I

THE NIGERIAN OBSERVER

Vol. 1. No. 104.   THURSDAY, SEPTEMBER 26, 1968.

top

REGISTRATION
capital of the F
Catholic School, :
announced in La;
The announc
vernment has pro
rest houses in the

BBC MAN JOINS REBELS

MR. F r e d r i c k
Forsythe former
BBC correspondent
and commentator on
Nigerian affairs who
was based in Lagos
for many months has
now joined the rebel
army as a major.
**This information was
confirmed by Angus Mc-
Dermid current BBC cor-
respondent based in Lagos,
during his visit to Benin
with the foreign observer
force.**
W h e n with BBC (in
L a g o s) Mr. Forsythe
while running comment-
ries on the Nigerian situation showed much inte-
rest in supporting the rebels, t h e r e b y winning
British public sympathy
for them.
Mr. Forsyth has since
resigned from the BBC.
Mr. McDermid w a s
unable to say whether
Mr. Forsythe w a s a
major with the rebels or
not.

REBEI DECII NOW (

**IN a matter of DAYS the rebels will hav
four decisions . . . . . .
Because Major General Gowon has gi
that the airstrip at Uli-Ihiala (rebel-he:
taken at all costs.**
The airstrip is one of 'biafra's' only remainir
side world.
It's liberation by Federal troops will not leav
sources of relief, because the Federal Governme
ling in food and supplies to liberated areas.
**Also, Lord Shepherd has arrived in Lagos to talk with t
vernment about relief for war victims.**
**Reports from Britain say that no one is now left in dou
is close at hand.**

This view is truly re-
presentative of world
opinion . . .
And this is why the
rebels have to make up
their minds. NOW about
one of the following four

points:
1) A fight to finish —
which can only make
their position worse.
2) Surrender — uncondi-
tionally (hoping for the
best — which the Fe-

Speculation about the activities of Frederick Forsyth was not confined
to Nigeria. *The Times* initially reported that it was widely believed in the
BBC that he was a public relations adviser to the Biafran government.
Later, journalists returning from Biafra were asked by BBC officials
whether they had seen Forsyth in uniform.

was pro-Biafra, but I was anti the fact that it was possible for a few mandarins who had never even been there to decide that self-loading rifles and mortars should be sent to an African general for use on villagers whom they'd never even seen. And then they should tell me that I wasn't to report it!

The second issue, of course, which applied to everyone once the famine began, was that no one, not even the hardest-nosed reporter in the world, can simply watch hundreds of thousands of tiny infants toddling to their deaths weighing a third of what they ought to weigh and remain unmoved. But that of course came later. At the outset it was not: 'I am here because I am dedicated to the idea that Biafra must remain independent'. On the contrary, I was dedicated to the idea that I will not be shut up by some guy in London who wants a K!

3 | The Propaganda War: Biafra 1968 – 70

Not long after Frederick Forsyth's return to Biafra in February 1968, the story started to change. The first puzzling signs of famine began to appear – images of famine that were to reveal the true scale of this 'small bush war' and transform it into a major front-page story in the west. Famine has struck countless communities throughout history, but the impact had always been local and gone largely unnoticed in the rest of the world. But perhaps this isolation could at last be swept away – if the media were prepared to take an interest.

The Biafran famine was caused directly by the civil war. It was a clear and unambiguous case of politics provoking a famine. Father Mike Doheny, an Irish Holy Ghost Father, who had lived as a missionary in Eastern Nigeria from 1945 to 1959, recalls:

> We'd never seen hunger, never. There was no shortage of food. People lived very simply, there was a lot of disease, but no starvation as such, and when we saw it for the first time, when we saw kwashiorkor, it really shocked us to our foundations. We weren't prepared for it and we couldn't understand it for a long time.

Kwashiorkor, a protein-deficiency disease principally affecting children, had arisen because of the blockade. Biafra had always been self-sufficient in fruit and carbohydrates, but used to import salt from Niger and protein in the form of meat from Northern Nigeria and stockfish (dried cod) from Scandinavia. When the war started the Nigerians imposed an economic blockade on Biafra. Opinions vary as to whether they deliberately tried to starve the Biafrans into submission, but certainly the supply of meat and salt stopped and a naval blockade prevented the import of stockfish by the traditional route.

Biafra couldn't export anything to earn hard cash either – apart from anything else, none of the merchant shipping companies could get insurance after Lagos and London had declared the area a war zone. Biafra responded by expanding its production of chickens and eggs, but this could not compensate for the loss, as the war progressed, of its most valuable food-producing regions. As these areas fell, there was a massive influx of refugees to the relative safety of the heartland, which only served to intensify the pressures on scarce resources. The result, by May 1968, was starvation.

One group of people who were immediately alert to the situation were the 200 Christian missionaries in Biafra, who were to play a key role in bringing the world's attention to the growing plight of Biafra's starving children. Eastern Nigeria had been a spectacularly successful mission area. The people had taken to education and Christianity avidly, and in return most missionaries felt a deep attachment to the Ibos. Soon after the war started, orthodox missionary work became impossible, with schools having to shut down because of the large number of refugees on the move as the war front constantly changed. Increasingly the missionaries devoted their attention to relief work, which meant getting food right into the bush villages and bringing the worst famine cases out to the feeding centres which they ran. Some of them even became involved in buying or hiring ships and planes to bring in vital supplies via Lisbon and São Tomé. Fr Mike Doheny explains:

> Suddenly we realised that we were all in the same boat with our people getting hammered. The children were starving and I realised for the first time the meaning of Paul's phrase: 'You are my children whom I have begotten in the Lord'. I had once taken that as a pious kind of statement, but now I realised that it was a fact. I was feeling: 'Here are children I have baptised, and here they are starving. They are mine, maybe in a very true sense. Even though it's not a natural child, it's a spiritual child, a reality.'
>
> And that's what drove us. And here were all these missionaries finding the same thing, their children were starving and so to help them they had to come together. And they came together not by talking but by doing. They started Joint Church Aid, which combined all their resources at São Tomé. They hired planes and pilots to fly them in overnight to Biafra.

Although missionaries are often portrayed as quiet and meek, they are usually strong-willed and highly-motivated people. Some of them also recognised the importance of using the presence of the journalists, who began flocking to Biafra once news of the famine broke, to publicise the plight of 'their' suffering people. Since many of them had lived there for decades, they knew the country and its people intimately. They had a strong infrastructure in place. Unlike visiting journalists, they knew their way about and what was going on. Their local knowledge was essential to the media.

Prominent among them was Fr Mike's brother, Fr Kevin Doheny, who had worked in Eastern Nigeria since 1954. He was particularly outspoken and journalists often sought him out precisely because he refused to mince his words. He was quoted in the *Daily Sketch* of 22 June 1968 as saying: 'I came here to help these people and will stay here until I am killed'. He brought many stories of the bombing of undefended villages and the like to the attention of Forsyth and other journalists. He recalls one occasion in 1969 when Mike Nicholson of ITN came out to Biafra:

Because of anti-British feeling, he wasn't allowed to take any photographs or any films. I asked the Ministry of Information if he could stay with me, and they said yes. He stayed with me in a house in Umuahia. We were there when the Ilyushin jets came right over our heads, strafing the church and the priest's house. Mike had his camera just at the right time in the right place, because the Catholic church was overlooking the town so he got marvellous film of the whole of the bombing episode.

While Fr Kevin operated in the bush, his brother Fr Mike spent much of the war shuttling in and out of Biafra in various liaison roles, sometimes on peace missions between the Biafrans and the Nigerians, sometimes spending days in inconspicuous Lisbon hotels helping organise clandestine relief flights, and occasionally having to travel in small planes full of stockfish.

He had been in the habit of shooting films since the early 1960s, mostly amateur efforts designed to drum up support back home in Ireland for his missionary work. Many of these films, he candidly admits, stretched the patience of even the most devout. But with the coming of war and famine, his films began to find a new outlet. The television news stations acquired an appetite for Biafra that was hard to satisfy. It was dangerous and expensive to put news crews in there, yet there was a public demand for more footage. The editors were glad of anything, and quite prepared to abandon their normal reluctance to use Super-8 film. Fr Mike happened to be present with his camera when the town of Owerri was recaptured from the Nigerians by Biafran troops in April 1969:

> I had taken shots of Owerri and the unfinished cathedral and the bishop's house with bullet holes and strafing marks on the walls. By this time I'd got to know a lot of these media guys; you'd meet them out there and they'd say: 'Give us a buzz when you're next in London'. They'd want to hear the latest news. So this time when I got to London, one of them asked if I had any film. He had a look at it and asked if he could use it. I said yes, on condition that I was in no way identified as the person who made it. It was a very delicate diplomatic situation at that time. That night it appeared on *News At Ten* which was OK, as they didn't identify me. But the following night RTE [Irish television] showed it, saying who I was, without so much as a 'by your leave'.

Fr Mike had reason to be worried, for there were threats that any such well-publicised activities on the Biafran side might result in the expulsion of all Catholic missionaries throughout Nigeria. Despite this threat, which was in fact never carried out, he and other missionaries were not deterred and they continued to do their best to exploit the media on behalf of the Biafran cause to which they were deeply committed.

Two wars were fought in Nigeria. The first was in the bush, which eventually the Federal side won. The second was conducted in the media, and there is no doubt that the Biafrans won that one hands down. The Ibos had dominated the Nigerian media and they were fully conscious of the need for publicity to attract outside support. Angus McDermid cites a British diplomat, who had once been a professional public relations practitioner, as saying, rather grudgingly, that in his opinion the Biafrans had mounted 'the most successful public relations campaign of all time'. They hired a Geneva-based PR company, Markpress, which also held the Chrysler account, to promote their cause. Markpress bombarded British MPs, newspaper editors, radio and television correspondents, businessmen and academics with over 700 press releases and other material during the war.

Even before the breakaway of Biafra, the Ibos' ability to handle the media was evident. These photographs, of Ojukwu (top) and Colin Legum of *The Observer* (bottom), are from the covers of the 32-page report of a press conference held in March 1967, at which Ojukwu, then Military Governor of the Eastern Region, attacked the Federal government.

The Catholic Church throughout the world also played an important role in the propaganda war. Since most Ibos were Catholic, it was natural for the Church to sympathise with them, and individuals like Fr Mike spared no effort to publicise the Biafran cause as widely as possible. In France, the combination of Catholicism and President de Gaulle's desire to weaken Nigeria, meant that the Biafrans got every support short of *de jure* recognition. In America, Senator Edward Kennedy, Chairman of the Senate Sub-committee on Refugees, helped to tilt official policy towards Biafra. In Ireland, Holland and Germany, there was also much support for Biafra.

The missionaries often talked of the conflict in terms of a 'Holy War' between Christianity and Islam. This was an over-simplification, which ignored the Christian belt in the largely Muslim north of Nigeria, and the fact that the predominantly Christian west supported the Federal side. But strong support for Federal Nigeria came in from the oil-rich Arab countries, while Egyptian pilots flew Russian-built Ilyushin jets for the Nigerians after Britain declined to do so, thus serving to enhance the notion of a Holy War.

When it came to television, the Biafrans were far more adept than the Nigerians. As Colin Legum of *The Observer* explains:

> The Biafrans stole a march by flying in everybody who wanted to come and taking them up and showing them everything. Thus much of the filming on television, which is what upset the Federals, was on the Biafran side, showing the devastation caus-ed, first by the air bombing and then later by the famine. So in that sense the reporting became one-sided because the Federals refused to let the cameras in, or placed great obstacles in the way.

The Nigerians in fact handled the media abysmally. They were defensive, secretive and very formal. They were reluctant to supply even the most basic information to the 20 or so journalists normal-ly based in Lagos and they made it almost impossible for them to get to the front. No army casualty lists were ever supplied. Angus McDermid's recollection is that 'you had to go round squeezing out news'. The Federal side had nothing to rival Markpress:

> The journalists relied heavily on what were laughingly called 'diplomatic sources'. We did the rounds of the embassies. We

tried to get stuff out of the Ministry of Defence, but there were very few regular press conferences, and the idea of daily press handouts was laughable. Scraps of information came from the generals who went out with the army and would give you a briefing when they got back. The government itself was very reluctant to say anything. You might get an individual soldier telling you something. It was extremely difficult and unsatisfactory; in fact it was an affront to our sense of professionalism.

For McDermid, it was of all his reporting jobs the most difficult to get anything absolute:

I used to amuse myself in the long nights by thinking about a situation and making a coefficient of reliability. Something that I gave ten points to, I had seen happen myself. Then gradually I worked down to things like 'who told me about this; what would his reason be for telling me? Have two people seen this?' and so on until you got down to about three, which was the rumour stage. It was a most weird task to report the war, and Markpress were no help; they were sending out disastrously incorrect stuff.

Forsyth agrees with this assessment of the Markpress bulletins. He 'very quickly came to regard them as being as foolish and as exaggerated and propagandist as the Federal bulletins.' But he was given far greater freedom than McDermid. When he returned as a freelance to Biafra, Ojukwu gave him accommodation, the loan of a Volkswagen Beetle and petrol vouchers, access to the one telex and freedom to travel where he liked, saying: 'If you want to get your head blown off, get your head blown off, but don't blame me!'

The problems of lack of information on the Federal side and deliberate misinformation on both sides were further compounded by the fact that it was virtually impossible for journalists to cover both sides of the war. Once you had gone to Biafra, you were automatically barred from Nigeria. Winston Churchill, then a special correspondent for *The Times*, did go to both sides, to Nigeria first and then to Biafra – but he would not have been allowed back into Nigeria again.

Eventually the Federals did give a small contract to a London PR firm, Galitzine Chant Russell, but that didn't change things very much because they continued to be very secretive and their army continued to behave 'pretty badly', according to Colin Legum. The

MARKPRESS
NEWS FEATURE SERVICE
BIAFRAN OVERSEAS PRESS DIVISION

136, Route de chêne 1224 Genève
Tel: 35 81 50 . Cable: BERNINC
Telex : 2 23 62
Daily Publication
Price Fr. 0.20

GEN - 657

FOR IMMEDIATE RELEASE

WILSON AND NIGERIAN GOVERNMENTS IN PLOT TO SEIZE AIRPORT

COPENHAGEN, DENMARK, JUNE 15, 1969 (BOPS) -- A British devised plot to deprive Biafra of the vital Uli airport was revealed here today by Biafra's Special Envoy and Head of the Ministry of Home Affairs, Mr. C. C. Mojekwu.

The plan, he said, was for the Nigerian's to harrass the Red Cross until it ceased operations in the area. Then, on the pretext that relief supplies had to be maintained, Her Majesty's Government could call on the R.A.F. to take Uli airport. Their excuse, Mr. Mojekwu added, would be that with the airport outside Biafran control, the flights could then continue without the risk of being shot at by Nigerian aircraft mistaking the relief planes for those carrying arms.

Mr. Mojekwu--who said that highly placed British sources had warned him of the plot during a recent visit to the U.S. -- added that the plan was obviously now being put into effect. He instanced both the expulsion from Nigeria of the distinguished Swiss ex-diplomat and Red Cross official, Mr. August Lindt, and the recent shooting down of a Red Cross relief plane.

The latter, Mr. Mojekwu described ..
Pointed out that that plot...

MARKPRESS
NEWS FEATURE SERVICE
BIAFRAN OVERSEAS PRESS

136, Route de chê
Tel: 35 81 50 C
Telex : 2 23 62

FOR IMMEDIATE RELEASE

BIAFRAN SUCCESSES IN SEVERAL

OWERRI, BIAFRA, JUNE 15, 1969 (BOPS) in the Elele and Owazza M the Biafran M made fresh gains in the recent day-long Ni Harcourt road war sector, despite a recent Okigwi sect announces. Despite in the positio all day last Thursday to consolidate their positio continuing to consolidate. Enemy offensives in continuing sectors. Enemy have been checked. Uzuakoli axis have been checked. southwest axis

In the Republic of Benin sector, in the river bank and territory, th miles of river bank and territory, th the area remains good, in Progress in the area remains good, in

The Biafran government employed a Geneva-based public relations company, which issued hundreds of press releases during the course of the war.

Nigerians constantly complained that they were getting a bad western press, and the issue soured Nigerian-British relations long after the end of the war, but they remained chronically incapable of remedying this situation.

In fact the western press was very much divided on the issue. It is interesting to note that Forsyth, who was pro-Biafran, and Legum, who was pro-Federal, both considered themselves to be in a minority. Because Legum had written so movingly about the atrocities committed against the Ibos in the North in 1966, he was regarded as pro-Biafran. In fact, he supported the Federal side, believing secession to be 'a nonsense which wouldn't work':

> I thought that in the end the Ibos would get clobbered. So I was caught between two stools. Because I was writing Federalism, the Biafrans weren't keen on me, and because I'd written about the persecution of the Ibos, the Federals weren't too keen either. So I had a difficult time.

The BBC was in a similar position. According to Angus McDermid:

> The Biafrans would have loved to have Freddie Forsyth stay on there for the BBC. And the fact that he was withdrawn and nobody else from the BBC replaced him, was a mortal blow to the Biafran cause. They were very bitter. They hated the BBC. And we weren't particularly liked on the Federal side either. You'd think that if you were hated by Biafra, you'd automatically have a position of privilege in Lagos. Not so, not so.

Journalists as a whole, Colin Legum believes, were totally divided:

> I'd have thought that the Federalists were in a minority. I was certainly having a difficult time in terms of the 'progressive lobby' of the Biafrans. I used to be trotted out as a minority view on the *Tonight* programme and *Panorama*. My ambivalent view was, yes, I'm on the side of the underdog, but in terms of political analysis, there's more to be said. Most journalists felt this ambivalence. Your heart was bleeding, but your head was telling you something different.

One journalist who particularly felt the ambivalence was Winston Churchill. A leader in *The Times* of 12 March 1969, based on 'our own certain knowledge', stated that Churchill 'started his visit to both sides with a pro-Federal rather than pro-Biafran sympathy,

though with an open mind. He retained this attitude until his visit
to Biafra.' Forsyth, who met him in Biafra, remembers:

> Winston had been given an absolute categorical assurance that
> there was no indiscriminate bombing whatsoever by Nigerian
> warplanes. It was all an Ojukwu-Forsyth lie. Then he saw a
> village wiped, absolutely wasted, by high-explosive anti-
> personnel 500-pounders from a high-flying Ilyushin. It was a
> village in which the weekly market had been going on, and there
> were some 500 women there in their gaily patterned robes with
> the children tucked in the back. What was left was just a charnel
> house. Winston arrived on the scene minutes afterwards. I do
> remember that his primary source of outrage wasn't the bomb,
> although he was disgusted by that. It was – 'They lied to me,
> they actually stood and faced me and lied to me'. I said:
> 'Winston, they do, you know!'

The great media breakthrough occurred in the summer of 1968,
almost by accident. Forsyth was then installed in a caravan with
access to Biafra's tenuous telex link, and was struggling to make
a living as a freelance writer for a range of national newspapers.
He recalls that, as with the missionaries, it took time for the full
implications of the famine to hit the journalists. The first
photographs, taken by the *Daily Express*'s David Cairns, were in
fact dismissed by his editor as mere Oxfam posters of no news value
or interest whatever to the British people. It was an assumption
that has often been made in such cases over the years but one that
has been proved wrong time and time again.

   In June 1968 a party of five journalists went out to Biafra at the
invitation of Markpress. It included Michael Leapman of the *Sun*,
then a very different paper. Leapman, 30 years old at the time,
had been with the *Sun* as *de facto* Commonwealth Correspondent
since the paper had replaced the *Daily Herald* in 1964. Before that
he had covered African and Commonwealth affairs for *The
Scotsman*. Leapman had been phoned up by his office on a Sunday and asked if he wanted to go out to Biafra. He agreed, and
flew out the following day with a photographer, Ronald Burton.
As far as Leapman was concerned, it was a war assignment:

> What I didn't know about, what nobody knew about at that time,
> was the famine. The Biafrans were not terribly keen to publicise
> it at the time. How we came to report the famine was absolute-

ly accidental. We'd spent about five days and done all the touring around. There wasn't all that much to write. We'd spoken to the people and we'd written the stories. The whole thrust of it was that they were showing us that they were resisting Nigeria, they were surviving independently, everything was fine, they were winning the war, etcetera. Then we were taken out to the airport to go. We waited for the plane and it didn't come, and about three in the morning they said: 'There's no plane tonight, go back'. So we did. If that plane had come, I would never have got the story at all, and probably never have gone back to Biafra.

The next day Leapman spoke to Alan Hart, then with ITN, who had arrived in Biafra a couple of weeks earlier. Hart had undergone much the same experience as Leapman. He had himself been about to leave when Fr Kevin had tapped him on the shoulder, said: 'You guys have missed everything' and taken him to the hospital to see the starving children. Hart duly made a film there and boasted of the fact to Leapman who made an immediate bee-line for the hospital with his photographer, realising that, since they were all waiting for the same plane, he stood a chance of scooping the story. That is exactly what happened. Ironically, the photographs of David Cairns of the *Express* had beaten both to the story by some weeks but his editor was not interested even when Cairns returned on the same plane as Leapman and Hart and warned him that others were about to break the story.

Leapman recalls his visit to the hospital:

It was the pictures that really made that first story, some marvellous pictures of kids in great distress. And talking to the doctor, who said: 'This one here is going to die tomorrow'. It was very moving stuff. I'd never done much of the heart-throbbing, sob-story stuff before; I'd been mainly in diplomatic reporting. I wrote down what he said and reported it back. And the *Sun* ran it as a series over about three days and sent me back about a week later!

It was at that time that I think the Biafrans realised that if they wanted to get the sympathy of the world, they could actually exploit this. And they did. They then took people around. But it wasn't their initial intention. They did that when they realised what the response was to that story, compared to the very limited response to the other stories that had been written.

Pictures taken by *Daily Express* photographer David Cairns were the first of the Biafran famine to reach Fleet Street, but were never used. The paper thought that the public would not be interested.

Leapman wrote his story in Biafra, but didn't telex it out because every night for four nights he went back to the airport expecting to catch a plane. Eventually one arrived and he got back to London. His first story appeared on the morning of 12 June, while Hart's ITN coverage went out that evening. Leapman's article was entitled 'The Land of No Hope' – a phrase which the *Sun* was to make great play with. The front page carried a picture of a child dying of hunger in a nurse's arms. On page two there was an article headed 'Why British arms count' about arms supplies to Nigeria, and a picture of Biafran soldiers with a case of British-made ammunition captured from the Nigerians. Page three carried a picture of a child in Queen Elizabeth Hospital, Umuahia, with a caption 'Boy suffering from malnutrition hides under a cot during an air raid'. This was later used in an appeal run by *The Times*, headed 'We can't sit and wait for a million people to die'.

Leapman's main report said that several thousand children had already died; that hundreds of thousands would starve to death that summer, and by August more than a million might be dead. The problem was exacerbated by the massive influx of refugees into an ever-diminishing area and by the Nigerian blockade. The hospital was receiving 2,500 malnutrition cases every week. Biafra needed 200 tons of protein daily, but was getting only 20 tons weekly. This report coincided with an emergency Commons debate on arms supplies to Nigeria, and copies of the *Sun* were sent to every MP. The next day a *Sun* editorial called for a massive international rescue operation and for more vigour by the British government.

A similar story appeared in the *Sun*'s rival, the *Daily Sketch*, on 17 June. Its front page carried a picture of a starving child and proclaimed 'Scandal of Biafra: the *Sketch* says the children need milk – Britain sends bullets.' The *Sketch* had decided to send out half a ton of full cream dried milk, enough to keep 200 children alive for just two weeks. It appealed for more. On 22 June Brian Dixon, who had followed in Leapman's footsteps to Biafra, filed a report in the *Sketch* under a heading 'Milk – not murder.' He described Biafra as 'today's Belsen', said he had seen 200 children dying that day, that those he had spoken to would probably not be alive by the time his report was read, and that nearly 3 million children were thought to be near death:

> The grey hair on their heads is the sign that there is no hope.
> The sign that they have a few days to live. They sit like decrepit

old men. Their bones are covered with only tightly stretched skin, their eyes bulge, and they look around them as if they know they are doomed.

Dixon quoted Fr Kevin Doheny as saying that the Biafrans did not trust any relief food which had been sent through Nigeria. He appealed for adventurous men to fly the food in. Everywhere Dixon went, everyone said the same thing: 'God bless the *Daily Sketch* for the milk you have sent and the people supporting your campaign.' The *Sketch*, which had already received hundreds of letters since its first appeal, now asked its readers 'to reach into your pockets for the children of Biafra.'

The *Sun* sent Michael Leapman back to Biafra within ten days to see if some way could be negotiated of getting food across the Nigeria-Biafra frontier. On 25 June Leapman reported, with a front-page picture: 'He's dead – the boy I saw alive only two weeks ago'. For day after day the *Sun* kept at it in an attempt to bring 'hope to the place we have called The Land of No Hope.'

There was an interesting assessment of this campaign by Peregrine Worsthorne, then Deputy Editor of the *Sunday Telegraph*, in the Granada television programme *What the Papers Say*. Worsthorne said that a letter in the *Telegraph* had drawn attention to the famine on 2 May, but five weeks then went by before the story was broken by the *Sun* and the *Sketch*. He continued:

How was the rest of the press covering the famine during these weeks of disaster? As far as I can discover, the rest of the press was scarcely covering it at all. The *Daily Express* had a man on the spot covering the fighting but not the famine. The quality heavies, *Telegraph*, *Times*, and *Guardian*, were reporting neither, at least from the Biafran side, presumably because they were unable to get anybody in to do the job.

This brings me to my point. The part which journalistic initiative, perseverance and determination still play not only in reporting events but in a sense in making history.

If the *Sun* and the *Sketch* hadn't succeeded in reporting the Biafran famine there would be no Biafran crisis today so far as the British public is concerned. In this crucial sense these two papers created the crisis or at least our awareness of it. For which they deserve great praise. (*Sun*, 13 July 1968).

Up to this point there had been comparatively little television coverage of the war because of the physical difficulties of filming in the bush and because the war itself was not really telegenic. There had been newspaper and radio reports, though nothing regular from Biafra after Forsyth's clash with the BBC. Now, in mid-1968, there were black and white photographs of starving children splashed over the front pages of two popular papers and there had been Alan Hart's report on ITN. The impact, according to Forsyth, was instant:

> Quite suddenly, bingo, we'd touched a nerve. Nobody in this country at that time had ever seen children looking like that. The last time the Brits had seen anything like that must have been the Belsen pictures. Even in Vietnam they didn't starve.

> Those first few pictures did it. There was suddenly a tidal wave of applications from Fleet Street to the little office the Biafrans maintained in London for space on a plane, for access. And then it all started. What they wrote shook the conscience of the world.

It was traditional newspaper journalism which made the initial breakthrough – the press had scooped television. Forsyth has his own view on what happened:

> At morning editorial conferences editors had been asking about the Biafran war, and diplomatic correspondents across Fleet Street had, by and large, been saying: 'I'm assured by my contacts that there is absolutely nothing there, it's no story.' And this was accepted. Only after those pictures appeared did the Fleet Street editors override the advice they were getting from the Commonwealth Office. Only at that point did they say: 'Bugger you, we are going to investigate'.

> And the guys they sent down weren't African experts, they were hard-nosed reporters, who went out with no prior conceptions or emotional baggage. They were just down there to report a story. And report it they did. With cameras. Then came the television and then came the foreigners. The war itself would never have set the Thames on fire, but the pictures of starving children put Biafra onto the front page of every British newspaper and from there to newspapers all over the world. People who couldn't fathom the political complexities of the war could easily grasp the wrong in a picture of a child dying of starvation.

Colin Legum believes that once the famine became an issue, this humanitarian concern took precedence over everything else, and someone like himself, who was trying to put across essentially political arguments in support of the Federal side, found it increasingly hard going.

The eventual breaking of the famine story provoked a massive popular campaign which began in Britain and spread quickly throughout the west. It was the first such campaign to be based on images of an African famine. The pictures of Biafran children clearly touched a sensitive spot. Forsyth himself declined to participate in this campaign, however, fearing that it might prejudice his independence as a journalist. Nevertheless he felt proud that:

> I was one of those who had made it an issue. Having done that, I didn't then become a flag-bearer or march at the head of processions. What I'd done really, or tried to do, was blow the story open, make them listen. And after that it became like a train. I merely stood on the siding and watched the damn thing roll.

It rolled with a vengeance following the appeals in the *Sun* and the *Daily Sketch*. Thousands of people in the west marched, protested and demonstrated, went on hunger strike, collected money, took out whole-page advertisements in newspapers and lobbied parliamentarians and other opinion-formers. Angus McDermid returned to London on one occasion to find a big pile of atrocity pictures on his desk, sent from a Dublin seminary, and a delegation from the Church of Scotland marching up the stairs to tell him what was wrong with his reporting! Even his own vicar chided him.

In June 1968 2,000 demonstrators in London fought police with 'fists, umbrellas and banners' and there were complaints of police intimidation. 'Support Biafra' committees sprang up everywhere, held meetings to pass on information from missionaries in the field, and petitioned the press and MPs. There was a powerful cross-party committee of MPs, involving Hugh Fraser, Jo Grimond and others, which lobbied for Biafra and put considerable pressure on the British government to modify its pro-Federal line.

Colin Legum recalls two powerful pro-Biafran pieces in *The Observer* by Conor Cruise O'Brien and by President Julius Nyerere of Tanzania, who wrote: 'If I'd been a Jew in Nazi Germany, I'd feel the same as an Ibo in Nigeria.' Young people everywhere volunteered to go out and help, while others offered to house

Biafran babies for as long as the war lasted. The campaign transcended traditional political boundaries. Young tories, socialists and liberals found common cause. Even the boys at Eton, the *Sun* reported on 26 June, had 'joined the growing campaign to help the people of Biafra, The Land of No Hope'. After being approached by an Old Etonian who had seen the suffering in Biafra, they had collected £200 towards the cost of the £1,200 appeal advertisement in *The Times*.

In western Europe too, Biafra became an important issue. In Holland and Belgium the pro-Biafran campaign, supported by the Catholic Church, forced changes in government policies of supplying arms to Nigeria. In France, where de Gaulle had his own reasons for wanting to undermine British influence in West Africa, the pro-Biafrans were spectacularly successful. In both Holland and Germany media coverage was largely pro-Biafran. In Ireland it was almost totally so. The Irish, with strong historical memories of famine in their own country, gave with stunning generosity. They have continued to do so. The American government, under attack from Edward Kennedy and the Catholic Church, began to waver as thousands of protesting letters poured into the State Department. In Britain, Harold Wilson and some of his colleagues faced personal abuse at home and abroad, and, as the death toll from the famine mounted, his government was forced onto the defensive. There were suggestions that, with an election coming up in the summer of 1970, the Nigerians would have to win the war before then or risk losing British support.

Churches of all denominations became involved in the campaign. The Catholic and Anglican Bishops of Owerri, in Biafra, launched a joint appeal in Ireland for £100,000 to send a shipload of food to the starving. This was thought to be absurdly ambitious. In the event, half a million pounds poured in. A boat, the *Columbcile*, was bought and others hired along with planes and pilots. A massive relief operation got underway, organised by the newly-formed Joint Church Aid.

After the first famine pictures were published in June 1968, journalists began flooding into Biafra and they naturally tended to check in with Forsyth as the resident expert:

> Each and every one of them impressed me by his complete unawareness of why the hell the whole thing had started in the first place. It seemed one couldn't begin to understand what was

going on, or why it was going on unless one could go back to colonial Nigeria and look at the first strains and tensions. So I got to a point in December 1968 when I thought it necessary to start explaining as best I could, and so I started at the beginning and began typing. It was going to be a long article, and then it became a pamphlet and finally it became a book.

I flew back to England in February 1969 with the manuscript to complete the two outstanding chapters, on the role of the British government and on Joint Church Aid. That on the role of the British government was obviously the most controversial chapter in the book. For that reason it had to be proved to the hilt, which is why there are so many references to actual Hansard extracts, which showed, I believed then and still believe now, that Wilson and his government were lying through their teeth, not once but repeatedly.

The Biafra Story came out as a Penguin Special on 29 June 1969 and sold its 30,000 print run in about four weeks. It caused some stir, and some fury in the Foreign and Commonwealth Office. *The Times* had a trenchant leader called 'A policy of famine', in which the British and Nigerian governments were roundly denounced for using famine as a war-winning policy and Biafra was described as 'the greatest tragedy or crime for which Britain has shared responsibility in this century, the worst since the Irish famine'.

With the book published and with the war almost over, Forsyth quit both Africa and journalism. The same pressures which had forced him to leave the BBC now conspired, he believes, to block his career. His friends in Fleet Street told him that he had no future there. The message 'don't touch Forsyth' came through to him very strongly when he returned finally in the winter of 1969:

At 3 am on New Year's Day, 1970, I remember staring up at the ceiling and the question that obviously had to be answered was, what the hell are you going to do now? You've blown it high, wide and handsome as regards established journalism. And back came the answer, well, you've got to do something old son. What about that story you remember all those years ago in Paris, the one about the rumour that the OAS might hire a killer to shoot Charles de Gaulle? Why don't you just sit down and write it? Maybe make a few bob.

And that was the impulse. I was literally broke, out of work, out of a flat, sleeping on a friend's couch. So I got on the typewriter that morning and in 35 days wrote *The Day of the Jackal*. Four publishers rejected it. Guys are still pointed out at cocktail parties on the publishing circuit as having turned it down!

There is an interesting irony here. Colin Legum, who had a high opinion of Forsyth as a journalist, is convinced that there was widespread admiration for his moral courage at resigning on an issue of principle and that he would, in fact, have had no difficulty in finding a job. Although they differed over Biafra, Legum says he would have supported him strongly had he applied to *The Observer*. He is further convinced, on the basis of 40 years' experience, that there was no way that the Foreign Office could 'black' any journalist in Fleet Street. He cites the case of Michael Leapman, whose pro-Biafran reports in the *Sun* certainly irritated the Foreign Office, but who subsequently worked for that most establishment of papers, *The Times*. Leapman endorses Legum's view of the matter. One can only speculate on what might have been . . .

But Forsyth was only one of many whose lives were transformed by the Biafran war. The Doheny brothers, for example, ceased being traditional missionaries and became intimately linked with Concern, founded shortly afterwards, which now plays an international role as a development and famine relief organisation. The experience they and others had acquired in Biafra was later put to good use in Bangladesh, Uganda, Ethiopia and elsewhere.

Similarly, a group of young scientists who had worked in Biafra, including John Seaman of Save the Children and John Rivers of the London School of Hygiene and Tropical Medicine, founded the International Disaster Institute. This began as a small, informal group, challenging some of the received wisdom of the relief agencies and seeking to promote a more scientific approach towards future disasters. There were many other effects. Monsignor Bruce Kent, for example, found that his experience of the Biafran war and famine was a major factor in his later involvement with CND. Michael Leapman won an award – Campaigning Journalist of the Year – for his stories from Biafra, which helped him move upmarket to a job with *The Times*. The journalist Auberon Waugh, a passionate supporter of the Ibo cause, named his daughter Biafra. And so the repercussions rippled out in many and diverse ways.

Father Kevin Doheny giving evidence to the US Senate Sub-committee on Refugees in Washington DC, January 1970.

Though Biafra was the first African famine to spark off a major popular campaign, it did not represent any long-lasting break-through in public consciousness. Having run its time as a story, it was replaced by the next drama of the day. It can best be seen as a one-off phenomenon which strongly influenced some individuals in the media, Forsyth pre-eminently, as well as some of a younger generation, like Jonathan Dimbleby, who would later make their mark.

Once the war was over, in January 1970, all the journalists were withdrawn and media attention quickly moved elsewhere. The Nigerian government was remarkably magnanimous in peace, and, in Colin Legum's view, never received sufficient credit for this. The wounds in fact healed remarkably quickly; Biafrans became Nigerians again with very little recrimination. Legum, in at the collapse, went to the barracks at Onitsha:

> There in the officers' barracks were the Biafran officers and the Federal officers drinking beer together as though it were

the end of a cricket match! They'd fought it very sternly and now they were chums again, as they'd been chums before. But there was another side to the affair. For the effects of the war-induced famine could not be erased at once, and children were still dying. The Nigerian government refused to allow the continuation of relief supplies from São Tomé or from Gabon and the Ivory Coast, which had both recognised Biafra. It insisted instead that everything go through Lagos, a much slower, overland route. So food and supplies lay rotting in São Tomé. Fr Mike Doheny believes that hundreds and possibly thousands of lives were lost as a result. He and Fr Kevin went to America to lobby people like Senators Edward Kennedy and Mike Mansfield in a desperate attempt to get the American government to pressure the Nigerians to open the old Biafran relief routes. They also saw the Canadian Prime Minister Pierre Trudeau and, later, Harold Wilson. But the Nigerians refused to budge.

Fr Mike made one last attempt to exploit his media connections:

I went back after the war, in September 1970, and I brought a camera with me and filmed a lot of stuff then. Alan Hart was extremely interested and we had actually prepared a film of the immediate post-war situation, about which the world was hearing nothing because the Nigerians didn't encourage any publicity at that stage. And this film was all prepared and was scheduled to go out on *Panorama*. And it was stopped by some pressure, I think from government. Alan phoned me to say he was sorry but it was all off.

That brought home to me how powerful this media thing could be – that they were so afraid of it.

4 | The Unknown Famine: Ethiopia 1973

In 1973, just over three years after the end of the Nigerian civil war, the world's attention was drawn once again to an appalling famine in Africa. This time the country was Ethiopia and the media person responsible was Jonathan Dimbleby. In contrast to Biafra, where newspapers had taken the leading role, this time television made the decisive breakthrough. But just as Forsyth's posting to Biafra and Leapman's stumbling across the famine there after his plane failed to arrive were quite accidental, so Dimbleby's film was made as a result of a haphazard chain of coincidence. Its ultimate impact, however, was stunning.

Ethiopia was then almost totally unknown in the west. Unlike Nigeria, it had never been a colony of a western power. People with long memories might recall 1935, the year when Mussolini invaded Ethiopia, trying to whip up popular support for his vision of reviving the glories of the Roman Empire. 275,000 Ethiopians died, some from the effects of outlawed poison gas. The world protested solemnly but did nothing and in consequence drifted closer to war. In 1941, during the Second World War, British troops drove the Italians out of a land they had never fully conquered. They took Emperor Haile Selassie from exile in Bath and restored him to his throne. That was the last time that Ethiopia was a story in the west until 1973, when the Emperor reappeared, this time cast more in the role of villain.

Before the revolution of 1974 Ethiopia was a backward, feudal country, barely in the 20th century at all. It was certainly a negative area as far as the media was concerned – much more so than Nigeria – and before Dimbleby it was not on the current affairs map at all. Foreigners were few and generally treated with suspicion. Escaping European colonisation – they had defeated an earlier invading Italian army in 1896 – had left the people proud of their independence but desperately short of such things as roads, schools and clinics. Like most African countries, Ethiopia has a poorly developed rural road network, though the brief Italian occupation did produce a few roads of high quality. The dramatic rugged mountains of the central highlands make transport and effective government difficult, as both Mussolini and Haile Selassie found to their cost.

The country embraces a diversity of people, including Christians, Muslims, pagans and even the famous 'black Jews', the Falashas, who were flown to Israel in late 1984 and early 1985. The Ethiopian Orthodox Church, the oldest established church in Christendom, dating back over 1,500 years, had survived, indeed thrived, despite centuries of isolation fron the rest of the Christian world. During the Middle Ages this isolation helped fuel rumours in the west of 'Prester John', a mythical Christian priest-king said to live somewhere in the east, who, westerners believed, would one day march in his armies to defend western Christendom against the Muslim hordes. From the 15th century it was thought that Prester John must be the ruler of Ethiopia.

The Ethiopian emperors had their myths too. They claimed direct descent from a line beginning in biblical times with Solomon and the Queen of Sheba. The Orthodox Church solemnly proclaimed their divine right to rule. So Haile Selassie was King of Kings, Lord of Lords, the Elect of God, Lion of Judah and much more. Such titles had once been common in Europe too, but in this century their nearest equivalents are those held by rulers like North Korea's Kim Il Sung or the late Shah of Iran.

Geographical and cultural isolation produced other strange phenomena. To this day, Ethiopia continues with the old Julian Calendar and is currently about eight years behind the rest of the world. It has 13 months to its year, including the short five-day month, Pagoumen. The tourist board urges visitors to enjoy 13 months of sunshine! Ethiopia celebrates Christmas and Easter at different times from the west, so the judicious traveller, like Bob Geldof, can enjoy two Christmases. The Ethiopian alphabet is unique. Even the hours of the day are different; the sun comes over the horizon to wake Ethiopians at 12 o'clock, and midday is at six o'clock.

Haile Selassie had presided over his country since 1916, first as Regent and then, from 1930, as Emperor, apart from the years of Italian occupation. A few western journalists, including the novelist

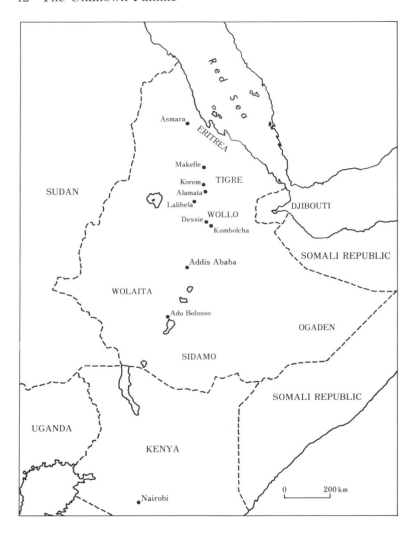

Ethiopia, showing places referred to in the text.

Evelyn Waugh, witnessed his coronation and had filed reports stressing the mysteries of a Christian kingdom with its own church and with little desire for what the west had to offer, including missionaries. Selassie, formerly Ras Tafari, became worshipped by followers of the Ras Tafarian movement, which began among black Jamaicans in the 1930s. Its origins owed much to the story that on a visit to Jamaica his arrival brought an end to a long drought. Ironically, Selassie's own end was to be hastened by another drought, this time in his own country. The Rastas saw him as a messiah who would lead all blacks back to the promised land of Africa.

He had enough problems on his hands ruling Ethiopia, however. This was no easy task, since the empire had doubled in size as a result of military conquests at the end of the 19th century, and the people in these areas frequently rebelled against the central government. Deals were struck with local aristocrats and despite a few tentative moves in the direction of democracy, the government remained essentially a feudal aristocracy which lived off the backs of peasants whom it exploited ruthlessly.

Famine had always been a problem – it is mentioned in the earliest historical records, dating back to the 9th century. There had been a famine in some part of the country in every decade of the 20th century. It was said that the people suffered their misfortunes with great dignity at such times. But callous rulers often say that of their people's suffering, and outsiders were appalled at the government's fatalism, apparent indifference and certain unwillingness to admit the fact when famine struck in 1972-3. The real miracle was – for all Haile Selassie's undoubted skill at divide and rule – that the system survived for as long as it did.

It began to creak as the Emperor approached his eightieth birthday and as superpower rivalry in the Horn of Africa, which borders the Red Sea and the Middle East, exacerbated regional tensions. At that time Ethiopia was firmly pro-western. The Americans had a satellite earth station in the country and agreed to train the Ethiopian army as part of the deal. They pumped more military aid into Ethiopia than to any other country in Africa. The Russians were in neighbouring and rival Somalia. The wars which wasted scarce resources were to come later. First, famine was to provide the catalyst to revolution.

Haile Selassie enjoyed a considerable international reputation.

This had originated with his appearance before the League of Nations in 1936 after the Italian invasion. It was maintained when he sent troops to fight in Korea in 1950 and became founder of the Organisation of African Unity in 1963. It was further enhanced by his mediation in the Nigerian civil war, in the crisis in the Congo and in the border conflict between Algeria and Morocco. As the 'Father of Africa' and the world's longest surviving ruler, Selassie's international reputation was regarded with pride by many Ethiopians and indeed by the Emperor himself. It is widely believed that he tried to buy himself a Nobel Peace Prize, splashing out a good deal of money on the French in particular. Critics charged that he cared more for his international reputation than about the future of his country. The significance of all this is that when his inept handling of the 1973 famine ruined his international standing, this undermined him internally as well.

The story of how that famine of 1973 was 'discovered' and exposed is a remarkable one. Jonathan Dimbleby was 29 at the time, the same age that Frederick Forsyth had been when he had first gone to Biafra. Dimbleby was equally determined and just as impatient of official cover-ups. As the son of Richard Dimbleby, Britain's most famous radio and television broadcaster of the 1940s and 1950s, and younger brother of David Dimbleby, who followed in his father's footsteps, Jonathan was clearly born with a microphone in his hand. After university he started as a radio reporter on *The World This Weekend* and then, in 1972, joined Thames Television's current affairs programme *This Week*. As a student at University College, London, Dimbleby had observed government attempts to muzzle independent voices during the Nigerian civil war and had drawn his own conclusions. He had also become vaguely interested in development issues, but because few in the media shared his enthusiasm at the time, he was careful to disguise it. As he puts it:

> Development was then a minority interest, and it was an interest that if you pushed too hard, could very rapidly make people say: 'Oh, he's just got an obsession.' I was very careful therefore to clothe my development curiosity within a much more traditional framework of 'here are major political issues at stake; here is a great drama taking place.'

The only African issues to figure at all prominently in 1972-3 were

Rhodesia and Uganda – Rhodesia because of the attempts to deal
with Ian Smith's white settler rebellion and Uganda because of Idi
Amin's reign of terror. Dimbleby reported both during 1972. In
fact, he asked to be sent to cover the Pearce Commission's work
in Rhodesia on his second day at Thames and found himself on
a plane the following evening! This was his first experience of the
living conditions of Third World peasants and he was startled by
the poverty and lack of resources and by the clear evidence of
malnutrition. He reflected that he had seen very little of this
reported on television. Rather, the staple fare from Africa was
nature programmes of the *Disappearing World* type or the occasional catastrophe story – notably the Biafran famine. Already he
had become critical of the prevailing view that Third World people were interesting only when they became victims of catastrophe.
Ironically, he was soon to become famous for exposing just such
a catastrophe story.

On a hunch, Dimbleby persuaded Thames to send him to West
Africa. This was the beginning of a trail which was soon to lead
him, quite fortuitously, to Ethiopia. He had read a brief newspaper
report of a drought afflicting the Sahel, the vast region stretching
across the continent immediately south of the Sahara Desert. He
didn't know exactly what was happening there, but felt something
might be wrong and wanted to go and find out. His earlier reports
from Rhodesia and Uganda had been regarded as successes and
so he had established some credit in the bank. He went off to
Senegal and after talking to people in Dakar for a few days and
doing a little travelling he returned to the capital:

> I found a telex saying: 'Is there story or not? Do you want crew?
> Let me know soonest'. So I got to the telex machine, thought:
> 'Is there a story or isn't there?' I had absolutely nothing fixed
> that we could film. I replied: 'Story on. Please send crew
> soonest'. Which is what in the business is called a flyer!

So the crew arrived and they and Dimbleby and an interpreter set
off 'literally on a voyage of discovery' upcountry. They found
drought, hunger, nomads leaving their normal grazing lands, and
large numbers of cattle dying or being sold because their owners
couldn't afford to keep them. They contrasted this, somewhat
crudely, with government attempts to build up a tourist industry,
and they raised questions about development priorities. It was the

first time such questions had been raised on television in relation to the Sahel. The film was beautifully shot and won awards for the camera work. It appeared in 30 minutes of prime time on *This Week* in June 1973. People responded with interest and it enhanced Dimbleby's reputation at Thames but had no immediate dramatic impact. However, as he recalls:

> At the beginning of September I got a telephone call from Holland from a Sri Lankan friend of mine, a niece of Mrs Bandaranaike, whom I'd been at university with. She'd happened to see my film on the Sahel. She was in touch with a lot of Ethiopian students in Holland who had been trying to persuade the Dutch that there was something terribly wrong in Ethiopia. They were being treated as if they were simply dissidents who didn't like the Emperor and wanted to cause trouble. So they'd made no headway. She was able to give me only the barest bones, which was that there was something very wrong. They didn't quite know what, but some students had been killed and there was a shortage of food and a drought in Wollo and the government was hushing it up and didn't want anyone to know. Was I interested?
>
> I didn't even know where Wollo was. Ethiopia existed for me, as for most other people, as a dramatic empire. So I went to John Edwards, my editor, and said: 'I don't know what this is, but if it's as it might be, it's clearly something that matters. What shall we do? I want us to do it.' And he said: 'OK, you can go and have a look.' He agreed partly, I think, because it's always good for a programme to break big stories, and so you're always looking for new stories, and partly because the programmes that I'd done in Africa before had worked.

So, as so often in the media, a dramatic decision was taken haphazardly, with no clear knowledge of what was involved and not an inkling of the eventual extraordinary consequences.

What Dimbleby and nearly everyone else in the west did not know at that stage was that there had been several consecutive years of poor rains and harvests in Wollo, where the local custom was for peasants to surrender 50-75 per cent of their crops to absentee landlords. Wollo was not Haile Selassie's favourite province – its peasants had spat on him when he fled from the Italians in 1936. The Ethiopian government had received many early warnings of the possibility of a severe famine, but had chosen to ignore them. It was proud, sensitive, afraid of losing face and resentful of all outside criticism. In particular, it didn't want anything to upset preparations for the lavish celebrations of the tenth anniversary of the founding of the OAU, due to be held in May 1973. The international organisations in the country, afraid of jeopardising their hard-won good relations with the government or of embarrassing the Emperor, agreed to go along with a shameful conspiracy of silence, to the extent of even covering up an outbreak of cholera, though they knew perfectly well what was going on. This whole sorry saga is fully documented in Jack Shepherd's *The Politics of Starvation* (1975).

The drought was the worst in the Horn of Africa since 1916 and was part of a phenomenon which had spread eastwards across the Sahel from Senegal to affect some 50 million people in many countries. The official line adopted was that until a government appealed for famine help, the international agencies could not volunteer it. Junior officials within both the Ethiopian government and the international organisations spoke out against this conspiracy of silence, but they were not listened to. The atmosphere of the time is well illustrated by the case of the United Nations Development Programme meeting held in Addis Ababa, the capital, to discuss the famine, at which the only record of the occasion was a list of names of those who were present. No further records were taken because people were so afraid of talking openly.

In February 1973 some 1,500 desperate peasants from Wollo staggered into Addis to explain how bad things were. They had eaten their seed grain and sold everything they possessed. They found a sympathetic audience among staff and students at the university, but were promptly sent packing by the police. In a rare example of efficiency, the government set up road blocks 30 miles outside the capital to turn back any more destitutes who might show such presumption. Those who couldn't make it home were dumped into makeshift camps where most of them died. Shortly afterwards there began a massive migration of tens of thousands of men from the highlands of Wollo down to the market towns along the main Addis-Asmara road. They were searching desperately for food and had left behind, in an even weaker condition, the women, the children and the elderly, many of whom were to die in their remote villages.

The missionaries, the aid workers and some government officials did what they could, opening 'feeding stations' and supplying medicine, but it was pitifully little. In mid-April, three university professors went out to Wollo to see things for themselves. They returned with a grim report and horrific photographs and were highly critical of the government for its inaction. University students then distributed their report and organised an exhibition of famine photographs. They resolved to forego their breakfasts and collected the money thus saved. They then sent out a delegation to distribute the money and interview the local governor-general. He was not impressed and called out his troops, who shot 17 students dead. It was reports of this incident which got back to Dimbleby.

By August it was estimated that over 100,000 people had died of starvation in Wollo. The international organisations were becoming increasingly concerned and asked the government to recognise the gravity of the famine and ask for help. Rather than acknowledge the situation and be embarrassed, the government advocated 'repentance and prayer' and chose to go without aid – and let its people die. It gambled on the late rains being plentiful enough to ease the situation and enable it not to lose face. The gamble failed disastrously.

That was the reality behind the unexpected phone call from Holland. At this time one serious attempt had been made to alert the attention of the media. Tony Hall, Oxfam's Field Information Officer in Eastern Africa, was sent out to Ethiopia with a photographer in August, a few weeks before Dimbleby, to check out alarming reports which were starting to come in from the field. Hall found:

> In many places, the first and probably the worst wave of the famine had peaked. As we started out, rains had already fallen, after three years of drought, and the countryside was actually green. Many thousands were already dead and buried; in some camps in Tigre and Wollo only the fitter survivors were in evidence.

> We rushed our material back to UK and waited in a feverish mood for the shocked reaction, convinced that this was quite shattering international news. But the news gatekeepers on this occasion could not give the prominence or make enough room for our coverage to do it justice. The only appropriate place that

week was already taken by a calamity in the Far East. The crisis quota had been filled.

The material was rushed over to another national weekly, where much of it was published as the lead item on page two. There were no big follow-ups, no signs of urgency in morning news conferences. We had failed to catch the wave. (*Africa Emergency Report*, September-October 1985).

It took television to catch the wave, as it did again in 1984. Meanwhile, because Dimbleby was already working on another project, he decided to send out a researcher, Peter Bluff, in advance:

We knew that we had to be extremely careful. The one thing you did not do was to go to the Ethiopian embassy and say: 'We've heard you've got a spot of famine trouble and we want to go and have a look at it.' We went in a very circumlocutory fashion and I wouldn't like to remember the words that I used too closely. I said we wanted to go to Ethiopia in order to look at this extraordinary culture and country and explore its achievements and problems.

Peter went out and he met Fr Kevin Doheny first of all. Kevin told him in essence that something was very wrong in Wollo, where he had been up and down in his Volkswagen Beetle, taking drugs and other supplies into the area.

Peter was extremely cautious and Kevin was also very cautious with him and very nervous because he was one of a handful of people who had just formed the Christian Relief Fund, which was very much a fledgeling organisation. He was terrified that because of the Ethiopian government's attitude he would be identified and the thing would come to a grinding halt, and what little was being done would be stopped.

Anyway, he gave Peter the names of contacts and pointed him in the direction of Wollo, where he knew the local priests and their concern for the starving people, and Peter took a two-day trip to Wollo and went to Dessie. He came back to Addis Ababa and telephoned me and said, speaking very obliquely because the assumption was that most telephone calls were overheard: 'I think what you want is here'. I said: 'Right, we'll come'.

The crucial factor at this point was clearly the presence of Fr Kevin Doheny, the outspoken Irish priest who had been so forcefully involved on behalf of the Biafran cause. After a dramatic escape from Biafra when it collapsed at the end of the civil war, and unable to return to Nigeria, Fr Kevin went to University College, Swansea for a year to take a Diploma in Community Development and Social Administration. He decided then that he would never go back to teaching again, but would devote the rest of his life to trying to help people who found themselves in the kind of desperate circumstances that the Biafrans had faced.

He was advised that Ethiopia 'might be a country where I could realise my aspirations'. He arrived in January 1972, not aware that a famine was imminent. He was involved first in development work in the south of the country, travelling to the missions and seeing where people could be best helped by water supplies and the like. He acted as a kind of broker for the missionaries with the aid agencies, whom he had first come to know in Biafra. Fr Kevin remembers:

> It had been getting bad in areas like Wollo and Tigre and I got to know about it and I went there. Then I was asked by the Catholic Church to open an office for welfare and development, which I started in March 1973, just before the famine broke. There I had a wider scope and I realised the famine was coming and I started to work in a very subdued kind of way because you couldn't talk about famine in those times – it was a very delicate subject. People were afraid. The attitude of the government was 'We've had famines in the past, so what's all the fuss about?' But things were getting gradually worse.
>
> I had some friends in government by this time. I was making my way through all these various government ministries and one day I went to visit two good friends who had helped me before. They confronted me and said: 'What is the Catholic Church doing for the famine? It is getting very bad'. I said: 'I'm glad to hear you speak about this, because I think we can do something, but I'm sure we can do more if we all join forces together and get the agencies and the churches working together.' I suggested that the Minister of Community Development and Social Affairs should call a meeting of the churches and I would supply names and addresses of people who could be invited. We could put it to the minister that we all wanted to help together. This was agreed.

Eventually a meeting was called on 15 May 1973 at 11 o'clock. I still remember that meeting very well because it was a very delicate one. And one of the most delicate parts of it was to get the permission of the minister to have our own independent meetings so that we could assess the situation and see how we could best address ourselves to it. So I asked the minister if it were possible for us to have a meeting, and he hesitated for a while, but eventually he said yes, and we promised to keep him informed.

After he left the room, we were about to disperse when I suggested that before we did so we should have an emergency meeting. So we arranged a meeting for ten o'clock on the following Saturday. Even the venue for the meeting became an issue; it was something they were afraid of. At that second meeting the churches were very cautious, and I remember that one church had a prepared statement saying that they did not want to belong to any formal organisation, if that's what we had in mind, but that they would be willing to distribute funds or relief supplies in order to reach the people. That illustrates the attitude of mind at the time.

This small pressure group called itself the Christian Relief Fund, now the Christian Relief and Development Agency (CRDA). It is still going strong. It was decided to hold regular meetings in order to co-ordinate efforts. These were to take place in Addis on the first Monday of each month, so that people could organise their trips to the capital for supplies, work permits and the like to co-incide with these meetings. Because of the prevailing climate, minutes were circulated privately. From a small beginning of half a dozen members, the CRDA has expanded to represent some 40 different agencies today. Fr Kevin, as one of the prime movers behind its formation, was anxious that some of the mistakes he had witnessed in Biafra should not be repeated in Ethiopia. In particular he was keen to find out exactly where the various churches were and what they were doing to avoid duplication of relief effort. Over the years the CRDA was to build up an important network for evaluating famine situations.

It was against this background that Jonathan Dimbleby flew out to Ethiopia in late September 1973 to make his fateful film.

5 | Television and Revolution: Ethiopia 1973 – 74

Jonathan Dimbleby spent a week knocking on ministerial doors in Addis Ababa before finally being given permission to film what the Ethiopian authorities coyly referred to as 'the problem of drought'. He retraced the steps of Fr Kevin and his researcher and travelled to Wollo Province some 200 miles north of the capital, accompanied by a somewhat nervous government guide. What he saw in six of the 'better' relief camps there appalled him. There were 13 camps in Wollo, holding in all about 14,000 people, who were dying at the rate of 700-1,000 per week from starvation or disease. There was a desperate shortage of drugs. The main camp at Dessie, guarded by the army, held nearly 4,000 people 'imprisoned by hunger'. It had no doctor, only one health officer, two nurses and five medical orderlies. They distributed what few drugs were available to those strong enough to reach the shack which served as a clinic. There was no sanitation and disease was spreading ferociously. At dawn and at dusk there was a round-up of the dead. Dimbleby later wrote:

> I walked through a series of huts where patients lie groaning, coughing and weeping, wrapped in rags, too weak to stand up, surrounded by their own vomit and waste. They are grotesquely over crowded. Typhus cases lie huddled side by side with cases of dysentery, gastro-enteritis, all types of fever, pneumonia, and tuberculosis. (*The Guardian*, 18 October 1973).

Dimbleby saw no doctors in any of the camps he visited. Oxfam reckoned that, taking the country as a whole, probably 500 people were dying every day. Perhaps 100,000 people had already died in Wollo alone, but nobody really knew for sure. Nearly 2 million people were affected by the famine in northern Ethiopia. Dimbleby was profoundly angered by the indifference of the government. He returned to Addis and telexed London for a film crew:

The crew came out and we filmed it all in about five or six days. And the images were pretty overwhelming. By this time word had got back to the government from our minder and from local officials that we had been filming sights that might be embarrassing for the regime. Our minder had started off trying to stop us filming things. He had said: 'Why are you always filming the bad scenes here?', and we had to spend almost the entire time pretending that the famine and these horrors were incidental to the 'reality' of Ethiopia.

Anyway, by the time we'd finished he was himself so horrified by what he'd experienced that he said to us: 'I don't care what you do, I want the world to know about this'. He also warned me that he didn't think that I'd be allowed to take the film out of the country.

There was an interesting reaction from junior officials in Wollo, who were amazed that Dimbleby had been given permission to film. They were afraid to speak openly, for they well remembered the shooting of the students, but they did say to him in private: 'This is very important, you must get this story and tell it to the world. It's very important that the world hears it'. Senior officials were a good deal less sympathetic however. As Dimbleby recalls:

I was summoned by the Minister of Information. He was a pretty impressive guy. About six-and-a-half feet tall, military, aquiline face, rather pale skinned. He was known to have a terrible temper. And he was in a rage, a suppressed rage. He said: 'You have been showing the dirt in Ethiopia. You have ignored the great things of this country. Why do you want to hurt Ethiopia? Why do you want to film these things? You have not done what you said you were going to do. I could stop you taking this film out of the country.'

So I thought, I'm being really bullied here. There was in the background the knowledge that Ethiopia in those days was a very brutal society and people could go to prison for a long time and be killed without too much difficulty, like the students in Dessie earlier in the year. And at the very least I thought that they could easily just confiscate the film or that an 'accident' might happen to it.

I thought, what tack do I take? Do I pretend that we haven't finished the film? Do we pretend that what we saw has been exaggerated? And I thought, no, it wouldn't work, since clearly all the officials up there had been on the line reporting back. And probably for the first time this man was discovering that there was something very wrong in Wollo. I suspect that Haile Selassie knew virtually nothing about this at all. He'd been insulated from any information because of a system of divide and rule – you keep trouble away from the boss if you possibly can – and none of the people in Wollo wanted the centre to think there was anything wrong; they were too frightened.

What I decided to do was to give him as good as he had given me. So I manufactured a towering rage, which is a craft I'm reasonably accomplished in. I was so angry at what I'd seen that it didn't take much for me to do it, but it was a controlled rage. I replied: 'That is outrageous. How dare you accuse me of showing the dirt about Ethiopia? I'm showing the plight of the citizens of Ethiopia, who, as you should know, are in dire circumstances in parts of the country, who could have help and assistance, who need not be dying, but who will die if help does not come soon.' I sat there, internally trembling. And he backed off and said: 'All right, if you really are trying to help Ethiopia then of course I will not impede you'.

Dimbleby was not reassured however. He went back to the hotel where he and the crew held a council of war about what to do with the 20 rolls of 16mm film sitting in their hotel room. Because, to his knowledge, there had been no filming in Ethiopia – except on flora and fauna – since *The Lion of Judah* in 1936, there was a lot of suspicion. He felt sure they were being watched, and decided to do a test run:

> I deputed Peter Bluff, the researcher, to go out with our unused film as if it were proper film. He went off to the airport and, as it happened, went through customs without any difficulty. We marked 'Ethiopian Drought' all over it so that anyone could see it; no secrecy of any kind. He took it out and had it stamped by customs. So we'd managed to get a lot of unused film out of the country! And we'd still damn well got the real film in the hotel!
>
> So I took it then. I decided we wouldn't go out with a mass crew, I'd just try to take it quietly on my own. I got to the airport and

discovered a terrible problem of getting on the plane because of some crisis of flights that I didn't understand. For the first and last time in my life I grabbed hold of the man behind the counter and forced my way through, I don't quite know how, saying: 'I'm getting on this flight. Here's the ticket. I want the seat.' I pulled the seat tab off and stuck it on my ticket. He was so shocked by this appalling behaviour that he obviously thought: 'I'd better let this lunatic have it, otherwise my life is going to be a misery'. So I got my seat and went through the departure lounge and no one took the film. And I thought, this is going to be OK.

I got on the plane. Taxied down to the end of the runway. Engines revved up. I began to relax, knowing that I now had the evidence. Roar of engines. Then everything died down. The plane turned round and came back. I thought: 'I've been rumbled. They're coming to take the film – and me. Oh my God!' Got back to the apron. The pilot came on and said: 'I'm very sorry we can't take off because we can't fly our route over Egypt – it appears that a war has broken out in the Middle East'. It was the very day [6 October 1973] of the outbreak of the Yom Kippur War.

Dimbleby had to sit in the airport for another six hours before getting a plane back to England. He had finally got the film out. Now he had to put it together. The film was screened on 18 October. Called *The Unknown Famine*, it is often referred to as *The Hidden Hunger*, the confusion arising from an article by Dimbleby which appeared on the same day under this title in *The Guardian*.

The major problem confronting Dimbleby had been how to present what was obviously going to be very controversial material:

I had to make a decision about what tone to adopt. John Edwards and I believed that it would be a mistake to be too accusatory. He felt that it was important simply to present the evidence of the catastrophe. I wanted the resources in Ethiopia that I felt were needed there because it was a real emergency. And I think those two views overlapped. I was absolutely clear in my own mind that the purpose of the film was to record what had happened. It took half an hour simply to report that powerfully enough to ensure that the film had an impact. To find out why it had happened, which is what I did in the next film, would have required more time. If I'd tried to build more of that into the film, I think the impact of the horror would have been diminished, and it seemed to me to be overwhelmingly important to convey that horror.

You have to constantly remember there was no prior knowledge of this event. It wasn't, as with Ethiopia in 1984, that people had a sense of things being wrong, or even had some perspective of a kind from which to understand famine. If we had made a film which was accusatory in form and concentrated on the cover-up, people would have been so revolted that they would have said: 'Well, we're not having anything to do with that. If people can't look after themselves, we don't want to know.' The degree of ignorance that one was having to confront in one's audience meant that we soft-pedalled that enormously. Other reporters would undoubtedly have gone for the cover-up as the 'story', but I think that would have been irresponsible.

Dimbleby had originally intended to include a comment that one day people would want to know how this tragedy had occurred, thus pointing an oblique finger at the Ethiopian government, but he finally decided to delete even that. The strongest political comment in the film was thus very mild. It ran:

This is the first time that the government of Ethiopia has allowed the outside world to witness this catastrophe. For six months, until now, it has remained a secret. The delay was fatal for thousands of people. The situation was out of control. But the government does now desperately seek the help of the outside world.

Even that was something of a pious hope, for the Ethiopian government immediately denounced the film vigorously! Dimbleby did however decide to adopt a more aggressive stance in his newspaper article, calculating that *The Guardian* readership was sufficiently broadminded to accept criticism of Haile Selassie and still respond generously. He wrote:

One day the Ethiopian government will have to explain why it chose to delay six months before allowing the world to know of this catastrophe. Were they ignorant of it until too late? If so they ignored the warnings that their own officials made last year. Were they then too busy preparing for the tenth anniver-

sary of the Organisation of African Unity, celebrated in Addis
Ababa last May? Or worse, did they know well what was happening in Wollo and Tigre and decide to keep it quiet? Whatever
the explanation, thousands of peasants have died and will die
unnecessarily. (*The Guardian*, 18 October 1973).

The Unknown Famine had much the same kind of electrifying
impact that the Mohamed Amin film, with Michael Buerk's
commentary, was to have in 1984. Even a decade later Peter Gill
of Thames Television, who also filmed the 1984 famine, found it
very nearly unwatchable and more gruesome than anything shown
in 1984. Dimbleby himself recalls:

> There was an immediate and dramatic response to the film. The
> phone was permanently jammed by viewers. ITN picked it up
> and used it in a news bulletin. People were deeply affected and
> shocked by what they saw. There was a groundswell of public
> compassion. We got onto the charities. Would they mount an
> appeal? They creaked into action – it took ages to organise and
> there was initially some reluctance because of bureaucratic pro-
> blems. I wrote an appeal.

> By this time the press was involved. I remember the *Sunday
> Mirror* started to organise its mercy lift – its front page was
> 'Did you see the programme on *This Week?*' and they took a
> big picture from the film. There were no other pictures available,
> so lots of our stills were taken by the newspapers and most car-
> ried a story of one kind or another. Later the RAF and the Army
> got mobilised in a limited fashion. Government mobilised itself
> in the person of Judith Hart, who came and saw the film and
> asked what was most needed, and I said transport. It was a kind
> of preview of what happened in 1984.

The Unknown Famine was immediately seen all over Europe.
Dimbleby, as the only person in the media with first-hand
knowledge of the famine, went onto public platforms and radio
stations round the world. Day after day he repeated the story. In
Ireland there was a massive response to a radio appeal put out by
Concern, which then sent a relief team to Ethiopia in November. Fr
Mike Doheny made a film of their experiences called *The Quality
of Mercy*, which was narrated by Cyril Cusack and was shown on
Irish television. It too had a big impact. The German magazine
Stern took photos from Dimbleby's film, did a huge spread and

then launched a relief operation of its own, buying helicopters from the money raised by its appeal. The joint BBC-ITV appeal raised £1.5 million, which was then a record, and so Dimbleby found himself supplanting the previous charities appeal record holder in *The Guinness Book of Records* – his father! By Christmas *The Unknown Famine* was estimated to have raised £15 million for various charities, a staggering sum for the time. The only exception to this generosity was America, then preoccupied with the Watergate affair, where the film was considered too 'downbeat' to be shown on television and the press never really caught up with the story. American government help was derisory and way behind that of *Stern* magazine.

The international relief effort which Dimbleby's film unleashed came too late to save the lives of over 200,000 people who had already died of starvation in the country as a whole. But it did prevent that horrific figure from rising still further as the area affected by famine widened. The relief effort, when it came, was not very efficient. It was considerably hampered by bureaucratic incompetence on the government side, and by rampant grain speculation by rich traders and by the Ethiopian Orthodox Church, which had also refused to take any part in Fr Kevin's relief efforts. A lot of people cynically made fortunes from famine aid. The missionaries and relief organisations lost out and had to pay over the odds for food. There was even enough grain in the country to have fed most of those who died, had the will existed. But landlords took the opportunity to buy land and livestock from starving peasants at knock-down prices.

One interesting spin-off from Dimbleby's film was the arrival of Mother Teresa, who wanted to send some of her Sisters to Ethiopia. They were not strictly qualified and so would not normally have been allowed to work in the country. Fr Kevin however was able to arrange for her to see Haile Selassie at very short notice. Like many before and after him, the Emperor was won over by her persuasiveness and gave her permission to bring in her Sisters. Fr Kevin, accustomed to the very slow wheels of the Ethiopian bureaucracy, was amazed at the speed of this 48-hour operation and saw it as a reflection of Mother Teresa's ability to break down all barriers in order to meet the needs of the poor.

The Unknown Famine served to stimulate discussion about the priorities for long-term development in the Sahel region. But its more immediate impact was felt within Ethiopia itself. There were many Ethiopian students abroad, like those in Holland mentioned earlier. They saw the film, were shocked and appalled like everyone else and wrote home telling friends and relatives all about it. In this way, and through foreign broadcasts and newspaper reports filtering through despite government censorship, knowledge of the famine gradually spread within the country, As Graham Hancock, formerly East African Correspondent of *The Economist*, says in his book:

> It was a curious irony of modern mass communication that Ethiopians in Addis Ababa thus learned about the starvation that was taking place in provinces just a few hundred kilometres to their north by means of second-hand information from those of their compatriots who had seen Dimbleby's film in Europe. (*Ethiopia: The Challenge of Hunger*, 1985).

The students were also angered by the crass response of their government. An envoy had been despatched to London to ask Dimbleby not to show his film. He was an urbane, westernised official, who now serves the Marxist government and who recognised that his mission was a complete waste of time. Then, after the film was shown, all Ethiopian ambassadors were instructed to deny that there was a famine; to say that the film had exaggerated 'the problem of drought'; that it constituted a scurrilous attack on the integrity of Ethiopia, and that it should not be believed. As Dimbleby says: 'It was the worst possible thing that they could have done, because it was so clearly incredible.' The Ethiopian ambassador in London was deeply embarrassed at having to go through such a charade. His government had never known such unfavourable coverage before and didn't know how to cope. Dimbleby's film had damaged its international reputation beyond repair. Its domestic credibility was also seriously undermined.

At the end of November 1973, just two months after Dimbleby's visit and a few weeks after announcing that everything was under control, Haile Selassie was persuaded to make a grand tour of Wollo, accompanied by 40 motor cars and numerous dignitaries. The relief camps were spruced up for the occasion. The Emperor professed great sadness at seeing such hardship and suffering. Now at last the famine was official and relief work could begin. The media was now free to report and film. At least 60 journalists and television crews surged into Wollo by mid-February 1974.

During 1974 the old regime in Ethiopia slowly crumbled in what was sometimes referred to as a 'creeping coup' because it took place so slowly. It began in January and February with minor army and air force mutinies in the provinces and with protests by taxi drivers, workers, teachers and students in Addis. Haile Selassie offered concessions and sacked his prime minister, but this merely produced a wave of urban strikes, demonstrations and boycotts, which gradually eroded the capacity of the old regime to resist. The local press, briefly freed, attacked the government for its handling of 'the problem of drought'. Government officials went on radio and television to deny the existence of the problem. But the 'mass media' in Ethiopia at this time was able to reach less than 25 per cent of the population.

As the central government began to lose control, peasants in the south took the opportunity to drive out the northern landlords and officials who had oppressed them for so long. Peasant soldiers, tired of fighting endless internal wars for miserable pay, began to molest and arrest their senior officers who had, by contrast, been lavishly rewarded by the Emperor. They seized on the growing evidence of the famine, knowing it was a weapon they could exploit to advantage since it revealed the cruelty, insensitivity and corruption of the old ruling class. These mutinies were warmly supported by many younger, junior officers who saw the prospect of quick promotion. It was they who formed the *Derg* (Committee), which took control of the armed forces in June and began to arrest senior officers and leading officials of the old regime, making the Emperor more and more isolated.

All this was happening in a frenzied atmosphere in which people felt free to talk and to criticise as never before. The famine was never far away from the surface of conversation because of rumours of what had really happened and because of all the visible signs of the huge international relief operation – lots of Europeans driving around with 'Oxfam' or 'Save the Children' on their Land Rovers, large numbers of planes flying in and so on. Famine refugees briefly camped in the grounds of parliament before being rudely despatched. The *Derg* set up a committee of inquiry to investigate officials held responsible for covering up the famine. It was headed by one of the three university professors who had gone out to Wollo the previous year and its hearings were broadcast and televised every day. Early in the year the Emperor had been spared personal criticism. Dimbleby, on a return visit in February, had been amazed in Addis to find everyone down on their knees with their foreheads on the ground while Haile Selassie's Rolls-Royce passed by. He was so embarrassed to be the only person standing up that he crouched down and pretended he had dropped something on the road! By August, the young army officers of the *Derg* had launched a daily propaganda campaign in the press and on radio against the Emperor and his alleged corruption. They found his former government collectively responsible for the disaster in Wollo.

At this point, with some 14 different political groups pouring out propaganda leaflets, posters began appearing all over the streets of Addis. Some showed Haile Selassie feeding meat to his dogs from a silver tray, next to pictures of starving peasants. There were also car stickers depicting the Emperor as a wolf in sheep's clothing, while others had his head emerging from a Belsen-like skeleton. By early September, partly to divert attention from other problems, the *Derg* prepared to deliver the final blow.

They decided on a brilliant *coup de théâtre*. On the night of 11 September 1973, the Ethiopian New Year, they decided to 'hang' the Emperor publicly on television. They mounted a 45-minute programme which comprised a bastardised version of Dimbleby's film *The Unknown Famine*, crudely cut and interspersed with locally-made films. The main one featured the notoriously ostentatious wedding reception of the daughter of a nobleman. The wedding cake had been flown in from London at a cost of £1,250. The film concentrated on the glittering elegance of the occasion. There were also shots of Haile Selassie feeding his dogs and of his large private zoo, coupled with allegations of corruption and nepotism. It was crude stuff, but effective. The populace had been invited to watch – as had the Emperor himself – and they flocked into the thousands of bars in Addis where people were used to watching football on television, and also into the main square, where a big cinema screen had been erected to give everyone a splendid view.

One person who witnessed this performance was Colin Legum of *The Observer*, whose regular annual visit to Ethiopia happened to coincide with the event. Legum watched the programme in a private house, with half a dozen leading government officials and academics. The effect was electric:

I was watching with the Governor of Gondar, who was, so far as I'd known in the past, a very loyal Haile Selassie man. But his radicalism, his hatred of the regime developed as the film went on. He got really passionate about it, and so did the other Ethiopians. They were all ready to go out and string up the Emperor. They went mad with joy and anger – a dramatic mixture of emotions. It made a tremendous impact.

I believe that theirs was a very typical response, because the next day, as one went out, it was as though something had been released, as though a boil had been pierced. It was suddenly all out in the open, the whole revolting business of the palace and the famine. All the feelings, all the grievances about the Emperor, got centred on the drought as symbolising all that was rotten about the regime.

Just after seven o'clock that next morning, Legum was woken by someone from the next room who had seen a group of soldiers take the Emperor away from his palace and drive him off to the army barracks. They had deliberately come in a small police Volkswagen Beetle in order to humiliate him. The front seat was pushed forward for him to climb into the back. As he was driven away, hundreds of young people ran alongside the car. He proffered a royal wave. They chanted back: 'You thief' and 'Hang the Emperor!' Not a finger was lifted in defence of a monarch who was once thought to be divine. His mystique had been thoroughly shattered. He died in prison a year later in suspicious circumstances.

This showing of the film was the first television evidence for Ethiopians of the appalling famine in their own country. Amazingly, Ethiopian television under the old regime had shot a film about the 'natural problem' of drought, but it was deemed too hot to screen and was probably destroyed. The bastardised film was, however, shown again and again and was also taken on a grand tour around the major towns and cities so that Dimbleby's face, in this somewhat disconcerting context, became extremely familiar. The film sparked an enormous debate in the local press, in the bars and everywhere else.

So Dimbleby's film, made as a result of a casual telephone conversation which itself only took place because his Sri Lankan friend had seen his earlier film on the Sahel, served, in this quite remarkable way, as a catalyst for the overthrow of the old regime in Ethiopia. The new regime promised better things, as all new regimes do. Optimists hoped that Ethiopia would never again have to endure such a cruel famine.

Like the one in Biafra, that famine of 1973 was generally regarded in the media as a one-off catastrophe, a terrible natural disaster compounded by the Ethiopian government's refusal to acknowledge its existence until thousands had died. It was not thought likely to recur and there was little appreciation of its possible long-term significance. However, there were people in the media who realised that the concern which it had aroused in the west could be exploited in a positive way, as did Jonathan Dimbleby:

> One of the principal effects of the catastrophe in Ethiopia, however crass it might appear, was that it provided an opportunity to talk about the issues of long-term development and the dilemmas posed by those issues. I was able to exploit that. People could now go to other areas of the world and make a film about the predicament of this or that place. I did it and other journalists, particularly in television, became very interested. People like Alan Horrocks, who now does education at Thames, a brilliant director.
>
> Other things happened too, like the emergence of the Independent Broadcasting Trust, which has had a great influence, and the emergence in 1979 of the lobby, in which I was centrally involved, which resulted in Channel 4 committing itself to development education as one of its essential tasks. There was now more public support, which itself had emerged from the effect of Ethiopia dripping slowly into the public consciousness. In the media it generally began to be realised that the issue of development could be interesting, and that it was possible to report it in such a way that an audience would be engaged and stimulated.
>
> I think that if you were to do a detailed tracer you would see a major upsurge from the beginning of the 1970s, which has been increasing steadily. A whole series began on the BBC devoted in one form or another to such questions. I was able in 1979 to make a series of films for peak-time television called *Jonathan Dimbleby in South America*. I went to Bolivia, Peru and Brazil, specifically choosing countries where there was no detectable

Jonathan Dimbleby (left) with director Ian Stuttard filming *Return to Ethiopia* for *This Week* in 1974.

story, but making three films for 8.30 pm for a mass audience about a tin mine in Bolivia, the impact of the so-called revolution in Peru, and of the plight of the inner city in São Paulo. That would not have been conceivable at the beginning of that decade. Now, if you look at the 1980s, you will find that lots of new series are being made.

I do think that Ethiopia, as a catastrophe that one was able to follow through, played a leading part in this major shift. I made about six more films on Ethiopia. The one about land reform, called *The Revolution is Declared*, opened doors to being much more serious about the underlying issues. These films were all shown to peak-time audiences of 10 million people. I think this meant that Ethiopia continued to impinge on the public mind in a way which was astonishingly disproportionate compared to the normal way that current affairs looks at the rest of the world – you go to a small country once or twice in a decade at most. What is distressing is how far behind governments in the west, and in Britain in particular, have been in utilising the residual interest and curiosity of their citizens.

Whilst this was happening in the media, there was also, briefly, considerable optimism about the prospects of long-term international development programmes which would reduce the risk of similar calamities recurring. Jonathan Dimbleby remembers:

From 1974 onwards, we had the kind of conversations that are being held now about the need for long-term development. I remember Kurt Waldheim, the United Nations Secretary-General, going in February 1974 to the Sahel and saying: 'The world has to unite behind a Marshall Plan for Africa'. I remember all the agencies speaking entirely in terms of trying to start long-term projects, going through their dilemma of how to raise funds for development, how to educate people into the recognition that development was at the core of the solution to the problem of famine. And I remember that a vast number of people would nod and say: 'Yes, yes we've got to do this, we've got to co-ordinate all the resources, we've got to overcome the problems'. And it petered out.

The tragedy is that the momentum that was undoubtedly there in 1974 and 1975 wasn't maintained. What happened was that food stocks went marginally up, people stopped looking like skeletons, though they went on dying from malnutrition, and the infant mortality rates continued. The people who were on the edge of the precipice and hadn't fallen over stayed where they were, ready to topple over next time around.

Thus, when famine struck again a decade later, it was as though no lessons had been learned. They had to be learned all over again.

On the day Haile Selassie was thrown into prison, the new revolutionary government took over in Ethiopia. Troubled years followed. Many long-needed reforms were carried through, especially of land tenure. Initially the new government enjoyed widespread popular support, but later there were bloody internal struggles for power. Dimbleby covered these traumatic years for *This Week*.

Dimbleby had returned to Ethiopia as a 'Hero of the Revolution', was greeted formally by the entire local press and television corps at the airport and had a street in Addis named after him. He found this intolerable, told them to stop as he couldn't operate as an independent reporter when treated as a demi-God. He was one of the very few western reporters allowed into the country as it veered more and more to the left. The last resident western correspondents were given 48 hours to quit in April 1977. Ethiopia became increasingly embroiled in wars against Somalia and secessionists in Eritrea and the Ogaden. At the end of 1976, in a dramatic *volte face*, Russia replaced America as the country's arms supplier. The whole Horn of Africa became involved in superpower rivalries and a crippling arms race which diverted scarce resources of men and money from desperately urgent problems of long-term development. Dimbleby reported these stresses and strains as objectively as he could.

His last film was on the savage 'Red Terror' of 1977-8, in which thousands were killed, including many of the country's most gifted young people. The families of those killed were not allowed to mourn publicly and they were obliged to pay £40 'bullet money' to retrieve the bodies. Children of 11 were forced to dig their own graves, and were then shot. The concluding words of his film were: 'Those who love Ethiopia will weep for the horrors of Red Terror.' The 'Hero of the Revolution' was banned. He has not been allowed to return since.

6 | Inside News

Tremendous changes have taken place in the media world since Jonathan Dimbleby made his influential film, and even more since Frederick Forsyth went to Biafra. At that time, most people in Europe still took their news primarily from newspapers and radio. Newspaper readership and radio audiences have both held up remarkably well since then, but by the time Mohamed Amin and Michael Buerk went out to report on another Ethiopian famine in 1984, most westerners had come to rely on television for their news. One reason why the Amin-Buerk film had such a strong impact was precisely because it was shown on BBC News.

The changes have stemmed from the advances in technology, which have not, of course, been confined to television, but have also affected radio and press. Whereas Angus McDermid in Lagos could only make contact with the BBC by calling from the transmitter at Radio Nigeria by previous appointment – with the censor checking through his script first – now the correspondent can talk from the telephone in a hotel bedroom in Addis, Beirut or Moscow. The mouthpiece can be unscrewed and connected to a better quality microphone or cassette recorder with simple crocodile clips. The result is superior speech quality and instant access to the main studio where the report can be relayed live or recorded onto a quarter-inch reel-to-reel tape recorder and easily edited.

In the press, changes include computer setting and the growing use of word processors at the writing and editing stage. Telephone lines can now be used to communicate text as digital information from a computer held by a reporter direct to the newspaper's computer, where it can immediately be handled by the sub-editors.

The most obvious changes which have affected television are the use of ENG and satellites. Electronic News Gathering is the name given to high quality video, using three-quarter-inch tape, which permits instant playback of pictures and sound. Satellites are now used routinely to send images across the world live into our sitting rooms – one striking manifestation was the Live Aid concert seen by millions around the world as it happened in 1985, while Sport Aid in May 1986 used 16 satellites to cover the Race Against Time events in over 200 towns worldwide. The extraordinary ability to see the Olympic Games or the World Cup or the deposing of Marcos in the Philippines, as they take place, is now taken for granted.

Satellites in conjunction with ENG have made much faster news and created an imperative – at least in the minds of those who put together the news in the west – that today's news must be shown today. The distinction is blurring between current affairs and news, as current affairs producers shrink their deadlines. This contrasts with an earlier style which more frequently allowed certain 'timeless' stories to go out as news several days after they had been shot. In 1973 Dimbleby's film, shown a leisurely two weeks after it had been made, still created a huge impact, whereas in 1984 the Amin-Buerk film – spurred by rivalry with other television channels as well as the desire for immediacy – was shown within 24 hours.

In the last decade the major reallocation of the roles of television, radio and newspapers has continued. Whereas once newspapers were regularly able to beat television to a story – as had been the case in 1968 when Michael Leapman had broken the news of the Biafran famine before Alan Hart's film on television – now the reverse is true, and newspapers often follow stories seen on television. Politicians have not been slow to notice this trend – developing television skills is now essential for the high-flier – and during elections in particular, it is the television reporters far more than radio or newspaper journalists who set the agendas. Even in simple career terms it it is notable that three of the individuals featured in this book – Jonathan Dimbleby, Michael Buerk and Peter Gill – began their career in radio or newspapers and then moved 'up' to television where the audiences are larger and the salaries generally higher.

In many Third World countries, however, where television either does not exist or is confined to the capital and a few major towns, radio is the main link with the outside world. BBC External Services compete with those of other countries – notably the USA, USSR, China and West Germany – for an audience of hundreds of millions. But the growing dominance of television news is a trend common to all industrialised countries. Mervyn Lane, Home Editor of ITN, describes television news as:

> Miniature films about news events, which have a beginning, a middle and an end. No matter what medium you do it in – you could do it in crayons for all it matters – the artistic idea of telling a little story in one minute 15 is still the same. It just becomes more complex with the change of technology.

However it remains the case that 'no video, no story' has become a cliché in the world of television newsgathering. Video, with its immediacy – no chemical process is required – has largely supplanted the 16mm film for newsgathering in the major European and American news stations. And it is cheaper. To purchase, process and print a 400 foot roll of 16mm colour film costs around £100 for 11 minutes. A video crew uses tape costing about £15 for 20 minutes. Mervyn Lane sums up the advantages:

> Speed and quality are the main differences. It looks nicer, it's more sensitive, easier to handle, easier to view, better in fading light. What it effectively means is that there's no such thing as a deadline anymore. In the old days of crackly stuff with holes down the edge, at eight o'clock in the evening it could be World War III and you couldn't cover it, and you couldn't get the stuff back or processed in time. Now, with electronics, if a bomb goes off in the wine bar at 10.27, you've got a fighting chance of getting the shot on the air. The pressure on the news editor of the day is infinitely greater than it was.

The use of video brings more freedom when it is needed. Film needs to be processed whereas an ENG operator is independent of the working hours of the laboratory – and during a revolution, the local laboratories aren't always open.

Youngsters are being brought up to see film as being old-fashioned and simply unnecessary, much as we look at valve radios, for all that they can be more powerful and offer a finer mellow sound with their speakers in solid wooden cabinets. And as Stewart Purvis, News Editor of *Channel 4 News*, says:

> Few who have used film and video will tell you that video has caught on because of its picture quality. In almost every respect, the picture quality is inferior to that of 35mm film. But video

enjoys advantages that film cannot offer. Not only is it more portable but it offers the major advantage of instant replay. That is a new concept that is not going to go away.

The electronic signal from video can be instantly transmitted through a network of land lines or microwave links. Microwaves, sent between the vertical dishes mounted on pylons or towers, often glimpsed from motorways, are capable of transmitting high-quality pictures, but can only work along the line of sight. Microwaves and land lines have, however, been complemented – and overtaken – by the use of satellites. These technological tin cans sitting 20,000 miles above us have had an impact on worldwide communications comparable to the invention of the telephone. Since the excitement of Russia's Sputnik in 1957 and the breakthrough in 1962 when the communications satellite Telstar's first transatlantic television pictures were received in Cornwall direct from Maine, satellites have played an increasing part in everyday activities. There are hundreds of them slipping through the heavens for a variety of reasons, many of which are highly suspect. Most are designed with one aim in mind, like meteorological studies, navigational assistance, or surveillance, while others are multi-functional.

Satellites used in television communications, capable of handling a number of channels, are stationary in relation to the earth. The small manoeuvres necessary to correct their wandering are countered by small gas jets controlled from satellite tracking stations positioned in a belt around the earth. The satellites, which last only a few years, act as giant relays, receiving and transmitting signals onwards by means of the transponders – the parts leased by television station operators for large sums of money: ten minutes' use of a satellite can cost £600-£3000 – ten minutes' use of a landline is nearer £100.

Early satellites' use was restricted to times when they passed within range of the receiving ground dishes, and tracking them was no easy matter. Now the 24-hour service of the BrightStar network of communications satellites links many European cities with London and American cities with New York and Washington and then on into the Main Path – a transmission motorway linking the three centres. By this means it is possible for a transmission from Europe to be received by several North American destinations simultaneously.

Satellites in Europe are operated by Eutelsat, a consortium of

European government telecommunication departments with its headquarters in Paris. A striking example of worldwide co-operation is Intelsat, whose headquarters are in Washington: shareholders comprise over 100 countries, ranging from the USA, with 36 per cent, to Burkina Faso, with 0.05 per cent. The equivalent for the USSR and its allies is Intersputnik, while Arab-sat, owned by the Arab League, covers the North African and Middle East countries. And in the USA, where a freer system has prevailed, satellites are owned by organisations like RCA, Hughes and Western Union.

Scores of nations operate uplinks, the stations with the necessary equipment to transmit to the satellites, and more are able to receive images with the far simpler downlinks. Initially, satellite transmission required enormous ground stations with large dishes – now ITN and the BBC have mobile ground station vehicles which enable pictures to be transmitted from remote areas. So commonplace is satellite technology that it is now a simpler procedure to get a picture live from Washington to London over satellite than live from Edinburgh using the conventional terrestrial routes of microwave and cable. Even more oddly, in the USA it is common to use satellite connections to send television pictures very short distances. To send images just a few miles down the road, often they travel 20,000 miles up into space and 20,000 miles back.

This technology might seem to offer enrichment – there is a romantic view of satellites sitting lonely in the sky passing messages between civilisations, a world in which we can all be much better informed. Idealists might even hope that global television – a number of countries are already planning a 'World Service' – will make the world a safer and saner place, in the spirit of the BBC motto, 'Nation shall speak peace unto nation'. It doesn't seem to be working out that way, though the potential, as shown by the overwhelming public response to the 1984 Ethiopian famine films, certainly exists.

But in the relentless search for instant news, the messages being passed may be out of context, raw, or at least undigested. Even at times when instant news is a pressing requirement, a satellite link to a distant country, where television presentation and styles may differ, may not always provide the enlightenment sought. According to Stewart Purvis, on the day that Mrs Gandhi was assassinated, the satellite link with the Indian station brought little advantage, for all that it showed was a studio announcer reading long diatribes to camera, followed by a lot of library film. There was no coverage of what was happening in the streets.

Though we may on occasion note such differences in style, we generally have no idea of who are the originators of foreign news. We can tell that it was produced in, say, Libya or the Philippines, but television channels, anxious to preserve the illusion that they have a network of correspondents throughout the world, do not tell us how. In fact the increasing cost of maintaining television crews overseas, compared to the cost of access to satellite material, has meant severe reductions. Currently the BBC maintains six correspondents and ITN has cut back to three. These are based in Washington (two each for the BBC and ITN), Johannesburg (one each), Moscow, Cyprus (covering the Middle East) and Hong Kong (the Far East). TF1 of France has nine. The Russians have 30.

Other sources for news include direct swops with foreign television stations and the use of Eurovision (which also covers Israel and North Africa), a system for exchanging television stories. News may be supplied by CBS from its own programmes after they have been screened in America. Occasionally items are taken from the USA-based Cable News Network (CNN), the 24-hour satellite news service, which was alone in providing live coverage when the space shuttle *Challenger* blew up.

And there are contributions – important for all media – from freelance journalists. The story about the oil company sanctions-busting in Rhodesia, which ran in *The Sunday Times* in 1978 and led to awards for freelance journalists Martin Bailey and Bernard Rivers, is an example. And the same is true of television – as in the case of Paul Harrison's film on *Channel 4 News* in 1984.

Channel 4 News has a record of making use of freelance contributions. For example, Stewart Purvis was pleased that well before the changeover of power in Uganda in 1986 they had bought a film about former rebel leader Museveni, now President, shot among the rebels by a freelance. On occasion, the freelances win out, as in 1986 in the Philippines. According to Purvis, 'a lot of people got rich when Marcos left. We were buying footage from all sorts of people we had never heard of'.

But stories will usually tend to come to the viewer via one of the two major international television news agencies, Visnews and Worldwide Television News (WTN), both based in London. Purvis believes that:

The role of the agencies is a crucial thing which the domestic British audience has no idea exists, but it is the major force in deciding what ends up on television screens from abroad.

The role of agencies in the newspaper world has long been familiar to readers as stories from Reuters, Associated Press (AP) and other agencies are bylined. These agencies, known as 'the wires', have been around a long time. Agence France Presse (AFP) started in 1835, and was later joined in the field by AP and Reuters. AP, for example, now operates in 115 countries supplying stories to more than 13,000 newspaper and broadcasting outlets around the world.

Television agencies are less well known, though after Mohamed Amin brought pictures of the 1984 Ethiopian famine to screens in Britain and throughout the world, the name of Visnews may be more familiar. WTN and Visnews have offices close by Telecom Tower, to which they are connected for overland line feeds and satellite transmissions. Most of the foreign news seen on television screens throughout the world will at some stage have been processed in London.

The reasons for London being the centre for the dissemination of the world's news include the fact that it is in a time zone midway between the Occident and the Orient, and that virtually every international airline in the world passes through London. English is also the international language of communications and many overseas journalists do their initial training in London. Tim Arlott, News Editor of Visnews, has another reason:

> The two biggest news agencies in the world are in London because we have a tradition of objective news, and because we thought of it first.

WTN originated in the early days of ITN, which started operations in 1955. ITN began to syndicate news gathered by its own camera crews and later merged with United Press International to form UPITN. Reorganised in 1985 and renamed as Worldwide Television News, the agency still largely feeds the independent networks. WTN sends four or five satellite news packages a day from London, transferring news gathered worldwide from its 40 bureaux and network of stringers.

Visnews started in 1957 under the grandiose and forgettable title of the British Commonwealth International Television News Agency, whose aim was to provide film news coverage of and for the Commonwealth territories, but it has expanded to cover most of the world, supplying and collecting television news in 83 countries. It hopes soon to open bureaux in Moscow and Peking. Now the world's largest television news agency and video communications group, it was acquired by Reuters in 1985. Both WTN and Visnews have extensive libraries of videotape and film dating back to 1896 with film of the coronation of Tsar Nicholas II of Russia.

WTN and Visnews have slightly different customers as befits their upbringing, and, like the national networks, the two multinational bodies compete fiercely to break news. WTN is more closely allied to the private networks like ABC and CNN in the USA and Channel 9 in Australia. Visnews has as its main clients the government or major networks such as NHK of Japan, ZDF in West Germany, NBC of America, TF1 in France and Globo in Brazil. Some of these are comparable to the BBC, with whom Visnews has long been associated. Not always amicably, as Tim Arlott explains:

> It's a slightly prickly relationship because they sometimes think that we are just a news gathering arm for them whereas we are constantly reminding them that we have 400 other customers. They phoned us up about the Royals in Nepal and we said we have absolutely zero interest in that; it's not a Visnews story, it's simply for the British. We have different news instincts, different goals and different audiences.

Visnews monitors television news from over 400 stations throughout the world and puts together about 40 stories of 90 seconds each from these – over half of them originating from outside the USA and Western Europe. They record the Chinese news bulletin every evening from Hong Kong and Arlott estimates that they have about two stories a week from China going out on their service, though rarely to the BBC.

The stories generally carry natural sound but no commentary, though background information is provided – which means that television stations are free to put their own interpretations on events. These are sent out in five daily satellite packages – chosen with the tastes and interests of the particular area in mind – to different parts of the world, including Asia and Eastern Europe.

Visnews has to be impartial. As Arlott points out, it is not in their interests to be otherwise:

> We are non-political, since we have satellites and syndication to Russia and the Eastern bloc. We have a satellite to nearly every Arab country, we have enormous customer blocks in Western Europe, the USA and Japan, but we also go to China, India and the Third World. Since our customers are everybody in the world we have a broad-ranging interest and we want to give as wide as possible a news coverage to all subscribers.

> There was one famous occasion when both Syria and Israel took objection to our coverage of a Middle East war. They both threatened to withdraw their contracts. The managing editor of the time sent the Israeli complaint to Syria and the Syrian complaint to the Israelis!

> We have to be straight down the middle. Of course what they do with it when they get it is a different matter, but we use no pejorative terms about anybody. There are no 'terrorists' in the Visnews world.

The actual treatment of the news may in fact vary from place to place, and tastes differ:

> If there is a train crash somewhere with lots of mangled bodies, some countries get very angry with us if we don't provide them with all the gore. So we shoot it and hand it over. The Spanish and South Americans will run anything. The BBC very carefully edit out anything that is not savoury for teatime.

> We are able to assign both sorts of stories. What the Third World regards as sensational, like someone jumping off the roof of a building, the Chinese regard as rather sad and can't understand why it is news. But for Australia or America and Japan, that's just a good picture. The Chinese, however, would consider people sitting round a table discussing famine an extremely important story. You would never get that running on Australian television or the BBC because they would say: 'Oh, a load of people sitting round a table. Who cares? If you want to sell us famine stories you've got to show us pictures like Mohamed Amin's from Ethiopia'.

Very rarely do the British networks give the origins of material they have collected from Visnews, WTN, or elsewhere. This is not necessarily a bad thing, but it might influence the ways we react to a story to be told, for example, that it is taken from an unfamiliar network or one subject to close government control. The average British viewer may never have heard of either Visnews or WTN and probably has no idea of their role in providing what goes out on the BBC or ITN.

The fact that national networks can now rely on the agencies for a regular, daily and painless diet of foreign news, which does not have to be fought for, has had at least two important repercussions. On the one hand it has produced a certain uniformity of foreign news coverage with identical pictures whizzing round the globe. As Stewart Purvis points out:

> Since the news agencies are putting out pictures which most countries are using, there is a kind of recycling of all the same pictures. And we have sometimes taken a satellite from another country to see our own pictures and thought: 'My God what's the point of that?' Quite often Israeli television coverage of Arab events comes from WTN's coverage so that you don't get any unique insight from watching their coverage of the Middle East. All you see is our pictures with a different commentary.

Secondly it has, in conjunction with the escalating cost of keeping correspondents and camera crew based abroad, resulted in their being whittled down, especially at ITN. The advantages of having foreign correspondents are great and sometimes overlooked by those in awe of the new technology. In Jonathan Dimbleby's words:

> Only correspondents on the ground can have a real feel for what is happening, have access to those in power – or those who might be coming into power, and report with confidence on developments in important parts of the world.

> The paradox is that we now have satellites which allow for instant transmission. What we are getting is fewer and fewer people going to places for shorter and shorter periods, where satellites can instantly transmit their undigested, instant assessment, frequently based on a piece of information that they've been given by some other colleague who also happens to have been there for rather a short time. So as we're technically capable of becoming more and more informed and better and better informed, we're at risk of becoming less and less informed by fewer and fewer people.

This also applies to newspapers, as Colin Legum points out:

> The specialisation has gone out of Fleet Street, with the exception of some Soviet and China specialists. One reason is the enormous cost of having foreign correspondents. When you slice up the budget between domestic, finance, sport and foreign, foreign comes below the line. So when papers are in trouble the cutdown is in foreign coverage. Sports coverage is equally costly but in terms of the struggle for circulation even among the serious papers, foreign news is way down the list compared with domestic news and sport. Murdoch once said that the Third World sells no newspapers.

The resident correspondent, who knew his patch, who had his contacts, who understood the politics and nuances of the situations, is being largely replaced in television news by a breed of reporter who is expert at getting in, summing up, and getting out of a situation fast. It is easy to contrast the worth of a careful story prepared say by Michael Buerk, resident in Johannesburg, on southern Africa, with an instant impression of a London-based correspondent fire-brigaded out to some unfamiliar part of the world which has suddenly spawned a story. The 'gangbang' syndrome has become familiar. Reagan decides to bomb Libya and suddenly hundreds of correspondents sharing the same hotels file almost the same stories compiled from the same sources.

How much research goes into the preparation for each trip will depend to a large degree on the amount of time available beforehand, and how seriously the correspondent tackles the subject. In time perhaps they will have travelled so much that they will have developed, willy-nilly, an expertise in certain areas. This is an intention of the editors, who appear conscious of the shortcomings of the methods they use, but are constrained by their budgets.

In Britain in particular the past 15 years or so have seen a sad decline in the quality of newspaper and to a lesser degree radio journalism in the serious coverage of foreign news. Some would attribute this to the influence of television. It doesn't really matter who is to 'blame': the reality is that both the 'heavies' and the tabloids are now far more trivial than they once were. Newspaper barons tell us this is what we want or what we deserve. The comparison between the way the popular press handled the Ethiopian famine of 1984 – pretty woefully in the opinion of

Thames Television journalist Peter Gill – in contrast to its handling of the Biafran famine, suggests that we have regressed rather than advanced. Similarly, people in the BBC's External Services argue that while they continue to treat their listeners as adults, their colleagues in domestic radio do not. So for Jonathan Dimbleby:

> You listen to a BBC World Service bulletin and you find out what's happening in the world. Listen to a BBC or ITN news bulletin, and you discover what's happening in the rest of the world *only* if there has been a major disaster, a megadeath of some type, the overthrow of a government, or a visit by the British royal family. So you get very little considered news. It's very depressing, and increasingly it's almost impossible for me to understand the criteria which determine the news agenda.

It is certainly ironic that an African schoolteacher in a bush school who listens to the BBC World Service news will be infinitely better informed about the world than Britons who get all their news from television. The latter will, however, know a great deal more about the lives of the British royal family. The increasing trivialisation of the media can also be seen in the replacement of early evening current affairs programmes by chat shows, quiz games and soaps.

Part of the problem perhaps relates to the new technology. Because television stations now receive so much material by satellite there is a tendency to follow the American pattern and to make items shorter and shorter. The American norm is now 'one minute 15' per item. American television recently found that Prince Charles was speaking in sentences that were far too long for such a format so the coverage of him was limited. British television is gradually following this trend towards 'faster' news, with the notable exception of the 50-minute bulletin of *Channel 4 News*, whose editor Stewart Purvis underlines the conflict of the new technology:

> It has revolutionised television news, but it's a double-edged sword. It has enabled us to do on-the-day news but at a helluva cost. What is tending to happen is that the cost of the big stories is so enormous in this competitive business that it doesn't leave a lot of money for what some people would call second-division stories, but what we would call fascinating middle-ground stories. By the time you've covered an Olympic Games and a royal tour, you've spent a lot of money and you're not looking to say: 'Let's go and have a look at Africa.'

7 | News of Africa

Africa has always been a most difficult continent for the media to operate in. There are a number of obstacles of a political, economic and climatic nature, but the most formidable is Africa's technological backwardness. Many facilities taken for granted in the west are frequently lacking in Africa. Electricity is generally not available outside the main towns and often erratic within them. Thus, for example, Mohamed Amin was unable to recharge his camera batteries when filming the Ethiopian famine in 1984. Distances are immense for those accustomed to European scales and communications are generally poor. Transport is expensive and often hard to obtain. The oil price rise of the early 1970s was upsetting for the west but truly devastating for African and other Third World countries which were not oil producers. Among many effects, it has meant decreased bus, lorry and rail transport to remote areas. Towns which were once on the airlines' map are there no longer. Compounding such problems are the civil wars which ravage Ethiopia, Chad, southern Africa and other parts of the continent. They may – or may not – provide good stories, but they also make life extremely hazardous for camera crews.

Television is either entirely absent or else confined to the capital and the major towns, so radio continues to be the main source of outside information for the vast majority of rural Africans. They often have a bewildering choice, as international stations compete for their ears – and their hearts and minds. The South African Broadcasting Corporation beams far up to the north, subtly wrapping its propaganda within some excellent pop music which the Russians and Chinese have difficulty competing with. Not surprisingly, the first objective of any group trying to stage a coup in an African state is usually to seize the radio station, which is the most obvious source of power. There's been a lot of blood spilt on the floors of Africa's radio stations over the past 25 years.

Africa

There are satellite stations in many African countries, but they tend to be underused. North Africa is linked into Arabsat, but in Africa south of the Sahara the links are more scattered. In Addis Ababa, in Ethiopia, there is a station which can receive but is not used to transmit. There is another in Harare, in Zimbabwe, which had serious teething problems, and there are a number of others whose performance is erratic. Some countries subscribe to Visnews and take its daily satellited news packages, but the number has dwindled in recent years. They can no longer afford what is seen as a luxury.

In practice Johannesburg, in South Africa, and Nairobi, in Kenya, two of the most westernised cities on the continent, dominate Africa's satellite links with the English-speaking world. Both offer sophisticated technical and repair back-up services. The foreign press corps in Johannesburg, attracted by escalating violence and revolt in a deeply troubled country, numbered about 150 in mid-1986 – the largest in Africa. It includes resident television correspondents of the BBC and ITN. In Nairobi there is a much smaller corps. Correspondents based there try to cover the whole of East Africa and the Horn of Africa, including Ethiopia. There are suggestions that since Nairobi is such a comfortable billet, resident correspondents are somewhat restrained in their criticism of the Kenyan government, in case they find themselves booted out and sent somewhere hotter and less pleasant.

Most African governments, whatever their political persuasion, tend to view the western media with mistrust. They may be afraid that their own inadequacies or crimes will be exposed; they may feel the media simplifies or trivialises complex issues; and sometimes they may suspect so-called journalists of being involved in espionage. The white settler-ruled countries of southern Africa always had a sensitive relationship with the western media, which they suspected of fomenting black revolt, while Marxist Ethiopia has banned journalists of the stature of Jonathan Dimbleby and Colin Legum.

Western press reporting of black Africa has declined since the late 1960s. The number of Africa or Commonwealth correspondents in both the serious and the tabloid newspapers, extensive in the early 1960s, has dwindled almost to zero, in contrast, Colin Legum says, to the French and Scandinavian papers. Legum bemoans the change:

In the '50s, when we still had serious newspapers in this country, I was appointed Africa Correspondent of *The Observer*. We built up a group of 12 well-informed Third World correspondents. We had an Africa circle, in which correspondents, editors and people from the BBC used to meet monthly in the Reform Club, looking at and discussing Africa. There was then a real and serious interest in it. Even the *Daily Mail* in those days had an Africa Correspondent. Now there are almost none.

Though the coverage is declining, the interest, Legum believes, is still there. In support of that, he says he has often been asked what has happened to Tanzania's ex-president Julius Nyerere. He is sure that 20 years ago journalists would certainly have gone to Nyerere on his retirement and sought his views on a whole range of issues.

Television coverage of the African continent, apart from South Africa, has also tended to diminish in the last few years. Television reporters are fire-brigaded out if a story is thought big enough. These have included Ugandan atrocity stories, the coronation of Jean-Bédel Bokassa of the Central African 'Empire', and the Ethiopian famine of 1984. The point worth emphasising is that only the spectacular, the bizarre or the truly horrific tend to reach our screens, thus reinforcing our stereotypes of Africa and Africans. The public may be forgiven for believing that Africa consists solely of Ethiopia and South Africa. We get no regular, routine political or economic television news coverage of Africa because of the expense of sending film crews abroad. So we have no context in which to place these exceptional stories when they break from time to time. Quite often we only see African countries in the wake of some royal tour; for example by Princess Anne on behalf of the Save the Children Fund.

Quite distinct from, but in some senses reinforcing these trends, is the decline in African studies in higher education in Britain. Those with expertise who retire are not being replaced, and Britain's once unrivalled academic knowledge of Africa is slowly diminishing.

The decline in information is not one-sided. As western newspaper and television coverage of Africa as a whole has decreased, so African television coverage of the rest of the world, never extensive, has also lessened. Kevin Hamilton, Managing Editor of Visnews, explains:

In the late '60s and early '70s Africa was an enormous strength in Visnews terms. By then every single country that had television in Africa subscribed. We had 40-50 stringers scattered around the continent. We had a desk which concentrated purely on Africa. It had its own budget. Stories would be assigned which we knew would not be of interest to anywhere other than Africa, and we syndicated those stories back to Africa.

But frankly the rest of the world at that point was interested in Africa only if there was a Congo in '64 or a UDI in '65. One by one our African subscribers started running into hardcurrency problems. The copper boom collapsed. Ultimately it got to the point where there were countries that had not paid their subscriptions to Visnews for five years and we were still going on sending them the service. Eventually we had to stop.

Very recently there has been a partial recovery, with Zambia and Zimbabwe starting to take Visnews' daily satellite feed and Zaire about to do so. Not surprisingly, South Africa was the first country in Africa to take this, in 1981. The 13 countries which do subscribe are: Algeria, Egypt, Libya, Morocco and Tunisia in North Africa; Cameroon and Gabon in West Africa; Ethiopia and Kenya in Eastern Africa; and Namibia, South Africa (including the 'homeland' of Bophuthatswana), Zambia and Zimbabwe in southern Africa. On the whole it tends to be one-way traffic, with no systematic offering of news from African countries.

One understandable legacy of colonialism is exemplified by the fact that when French television shows something on Africa, it tends to be on a French-speaking country, while in Portugal the main focus is on Angola and Mozambique. It is not therefore surprising that in Britain we rarely hear much about French-speaking Chad, a country with desperate problems. Ethiopia, which was nobody's colony, is an exception to this pattern and one which owes much to Jonathan Dimbleby's original association with the country.

An explanation for the relative lack of media coverage of Africa is often sought in terms of the difficulty of access. There can indeed be problems over visas, as would be the case in Ethiopia in August and September 1984. This particularly affects television, with its need to take out camera crews in a hurry, as Maggie Eales, Senior Foreign Editor of ITN, explains:

When we know a certain part of the world is in for a bumpy

time, we try and make sure that a variety of crews have got visas. There'd be enough people visa-ed up so that at seven o'clock on a Sunday morning you could find a crew. We've got to be on the ball, but of course we get caught out. If a story breaks on a Saturday night and the embassy doesn't open till Monday we have to wait till then to get the visas. Or else we have to weigh up if it's worth taking a flyer and getting on a plane – if they'll let you on without a visa.

But that is not easy, as Michael Buerk points out. When he returned to Ethiopia shortly after his report in October 1984 had sparked off an enormous response to aid the famine victims, he was accompanied by colleague Christopher Morris who had no visa. The Ethiopian authorities were unimpressed by his BBC credentials. 'They totally refused to give him a visa and flung him out!'

For newspaper and radio journalists, access can be slightly easier. Colin Legum, one of an older breed of African journalists, believes that the problem is often exaggerated but that it also stems from changing patterns of journalism:

Some countries, but not many, don't give easy access. You can count the countries with difficulty of access on the fingers of one hand. I can't go to Ethiopia but others can – it isn't closed to western correspondents. South Africa is difficult for a few people but not for many. Zimbabwe is open house, as is Kenya, Uganda, Tanzania, Nigeria, Ghana, Gambia, Senegal, Gabon and so on. It's a misapprehension; there is access. If you're an experienced person – and this is the point, you must have contacts – then you can get the story. If you haven't got the contacts and you go in as a greenhorn, and you don't know who to see and you haven't got reliable people, then you won't get your story.

Angus McDermid spent 12 years for the BBC in different parts of Africa, and I don't see that happening any more. Today's correspondents haven't built up relationships over a period of time. There are no young people going in. I think Paul Vallely is the brightest young star in the British journalistic firmament in the last five years. He was doing some brilliant reporting from Sudan and Ethiopia. If *The Times* had left him in the Horn of Africa and extended his scope slightly, he could have built up the sort of relationships over the years that many of us had in the past.

It takes a long time. But now he's being restricted to domestic stuff. It's all part of the loss of specialisation.

The arguments about the difficulties of filming in Africa can also be overstated. Jonathan Dimbleby, asked about the problems of sending crews out to Ethiopia and other African countries in the early 1970s, commented:

> It's not easy, of course, because transport is difficult to obtain, particularly if you have rather large camera crews. The conditions are unfamiliar to a crew when it first comes out. There are the usual problems of stomach upsets, dysentery, too much sun, having to work at a pace inappropriate for the heat and the climate, not having easy places to stay, and so on. It's not a comfortable life but it would be wrong to exaggerate the problems.

> In Ethiopia we had battery lights, which you had to charge up when you could on whatever mains supply was available. It was a problem, but the Wollo episode that we filmed was up and down the main road to Eritrea, with towns all the way along, providing very basic amenities, including electricity. So it was not as difficult as filming in Tanzania or subsequently in Ethiopia, when we went much further off the road, and then walked and used donkeys.

> Much more important are the political problems. My main anxiety in Ethiopia all the time was officials preventing me doing what I wanted to do and my entire energy was concentrated on getting round the restraints of frightened and very powerful officials.

Given the relative weakness of television links between Africa and the west, radio broadcasting remains of major significance. The transistor radio, which arrived in Africa in the early '60s, produced a revolution in communications. Earlier valve sets had required mains electricity which was simply not available in most places, and nationalist politicians seeking to exploit the media had to be content with newspapers.

The BBC's External Services now broadcast to the world in English and 36 other languages for 727 hours every week to a regular audience – people who listen at least once a week – estimated in 1986 at 120 million. India is the largest single audience, and more people listen to the BBC in Hindi (35 million) than listen in English worldwide (25 million). Africa takes a pretty hefty chunk of the BBC's audience, with Nigeria (15 million) being the second largest audience after India and ahead of Russia (14 million). The main service in English is the World Service, which operates around the clock, and is addressed to all different parts of the world at their peak listening times – early morning and early evening. It broadcasts 244 hours per week. There are a number of regional services, including African, Arabic, Far Eastern and Latin American, which produce programmes focusing on their particular area.

The Arabic, French and South European Services to Africa broadcast in Arabic (56 hours per week), French (23) and Portuguese (5). The African Service broadcasts in English and in three African languages: Hausa (9 hours) for West Africa, Swahili (7) for East Africa and Somali (7) for the Horn of Africa. The comparative figures for other countries broadcasting in these languages are as follows:

	Hours per week
Hausa	
USSR	18
West Germany	11
UK	9
China	7
USA	7
Swahili	
USSR	25
West Germany	19
China	10
Warsaw Pact	10
UK	7
USA	7
Somali	
UK	7
USSR	7

Back in 1950 the BBC External Services used to broadcast more
hours per week (643) to the world than any other station. Following on behind at that time were the USSR (533) and the USA (497).
By 1955 the UK had already slipped into third place behind the
two superpowers; by 1960 she was overtaken by China and by 1965
by West Germany. The figures in mid-1986 were:

Country	Hours per week
USA	2,339
USSR	2,211
China	1,446
West Germany	795
UK	726
Albania	581
Egypt	560
North Korea	535

The only other African countries to make the top 30 are Nigeria,
which is in 14th position, with 322 hours per week, and South
Africa, in 25th position, with 205 hours per week.

Currently BBC Radio has resident correspondents in four African
countries: Egypt, Ivory Coast, Kenya and South Africa. In addition
it has regular stringers in those countries plus Algeria, Morocco,
Sudan, Tunisia, Zambia and Zimbabwe. There is a stringer of some
kind in virtually every African country; normally a local journalist
who reports occasionally. Though no exclusivity is allowed within
the BBC, and any section is able to take material from any other,
reports from stringers in Africa tend to be heard only on the African
Service, and very rarely on domestic radio. A vast fund of
knowledge of Africa, garnered by the BBC, sadly never percolates
through to British audiences on the domestic wavelengths.

Since the mid-1970s, successive governments have imposed cuts
on the BBC's External Services. This is an absurdly short-sighted
policy, since the BBC, at very little cost, is one of Britain's finest
and most influential ambassadors. Thus far, the African Service
has escaped the brunt of these cuts. It has a wide and devoted
audience, especially because in most African countries radio and

The 'saucepan special' - the first popular mass-produced radio set in Africa. The idea of Harry Franklin, Director of Information and Broadcasting Services in Northern Rhodesia (now Zambia), it was developed by Ever Ready and introduced in 1949. At £5, plus 25 shillings for the battery, it undercut the cheapest alternative, which cost £45.

television are state controlled and very little, if anything, of an objective or anti-government nature is allowed on the air. So people often turn to the BBC for hard information, especially at times of local crisis. The BBC has retained an enviable reputation for accuracy and objectivity in Africa. Its news is even transported by word of mouth to those who cannot understand English, and correspondents like Angus McDermid, who reported from Africa for 12 years, gain a far wider reputation in Africa than they enjoy at home.

Graham Mytton, Head of International Broadcasting and Audience Research in the External Services, has wide experience of Africa and has worked in both external and home broadcasting. In his view:

> In the External Services, and in the African Service in particular, we treat our listeners much more seriously. We make far less allowance for lack of knowledge or not being up-to-date than any other part the BBC. And it pays off. We have an enthusiastic following, especially in West Africa, where the signal is very good. We don't steer away from stories just because we think our listeners won't understand them.

> Whereas I feel in domestic radio we are increasingly simplifying things. Our domestic channels don't challenge the stereotypes that people have of Africa very much; they tend to follow them.

Mytton believes that domestic radio feeds off newspapers to an unhealthy degree and does not do nearly enough homework. By contrast, African Service producers read the agency tapes (Agence France Presse, for example, is in 44 African countries) and listen to the monitoring stations – there is one in Nairobi covering the whole continent. 'We read all that; they don't in domestic', he says. The External Services' news and current affairs programmes are highly regarded in the media world. They are less parochial than the comparable domestic programmes and some argue that they are also more objective as well as being better informed. The fact that the World Service can now be heard – by mistake rather than design – at certain times of the day in Britain itself has gained it a new audience, driven away by the increasing trivialisation of domestic radio and television news.

News out of Africa has always tended to be erratic, though far less so in radio than television. In the late 1970s BBC TV had two foreign correspondents based in Africa, one in Kenya and the other in South Africa. Brian Barron was sent to Nairobi after working in Vietnam and as Far Eastern Correspondent in Hong Kong. It was thought that Nairobi might be a useful base from which to file stories on Idi Amin. Barron and David Smith of ITN competed fiercely to file horror stories of famine in northern Uganda. Eventually it was felt that these stories were becoming repetitive and, with Amin gone from the scene, though with no end in sight to Uganda's nightmare, it was decided not to keep the office open when Barron moved on.

That left only the Southern Africa desk, though domestic radio's Mike Wooldridge, who is based in Kenya, also does a certain amount of television work. The one country that Britain has consistently received news from, and continues to do so at a surprising rate, is South Africa. This is due more to the fact that English-speaking white people are involved and to the well-serviced satellite links than to the inherent worth of the story.

The BBC's Johannesburg office was opened in the mid-1970s, as a base from which to cover the escalating civil war in Rhodesia between the white settlers and the African nationalist guerrillas. The war finally ended when the country became independent as Zimbabwe in 1980. By 1983, the year Michael Buerk was sent to southern Africa, the BBC was thinking of closing the office down because there was little of interest to report from Zimbabwe, while South Africa seemed pretty quiet. Buerk managed to persuade them that South Africa was about to explode and that the desk should be retained. He succeeded.

Buerk's title is Southern Africa Correspondent. Working from his present home in Johannesburg, cottage-industry-style, he has increasingly found himself confined there, reporting South African stories. He does make occasional forays – in an average year, he goes to Mozambique five times, to Zambia once or twice, and once to southern Angola, to the part held by the American-backed Jonas Savimbi. The 'frontline' states which border South Africa, and often get raided by her, have decreed that no correspondents based in South Africa should be allowed to work in their countries. In practice only Zimbabwe, the prime instigator of the move, enforces this ban, and so he is unable to go there. So Buerk spends over 90 per cent of his time in South Africa.

He is reluctant to leave his base for any length of time in case really big stories break on his home patch. Political events move so fast and unpredictably that Buerk and his BBC crew often co-operate and share material with the three Visnews and three NBC crews operating in South Africa. He is expected to put together two or three detailed feature pieces each week, plus whatever spot stories happen to break. He edits from home and satellites from the South African Broadcasting Corporation to London at about £1,000 per transmission. How much of his material gets shown on the *Nine o'clock News* obviously depends on the amount of hot news coming into London that day from elsewhere.

In 1985 the South African government imposed emergency regulations in an attempt to muzzle foreign press reporting of grow-ing violence in the country. Buerk believes that these restrictions were only about 60 per cent effective, because it was in the nature of the violence in South Africa that it spread quickly and unpredict-ably, into and out of the areas covered by the emergency. But there were other difficulties, such as the police having more television cameras than the international press and plain clothes police claim-ing to be members of the press.

In covering riots Buerk, and other correspondents, often have the problem of knowing that they have filmed people committing illegal acts; of knowing that the security police have means of recor-ding what they send out, and that South African embassies abroad can easily monitor what goes out on the BBC and other networks; and that therefore what they film can be used to convict someone in court. Despite obvious examples of government pressures and abuse of police powers, it was Buerk's belief (at least before the increased restrictions imposed in June 1986) that:

> The freedom to report in South Africa is unique in Africa in my experience. The amount of interference, even by the police, is less than in most African countries I've ever worked in. By First World standards government toleration is not enough, but by Third World standards it's more than most other countries. It just depends on which scale of criteria you judge them by.

Buerk feels both isolated from blacks in South Africa by the apar-theid laws and distanced from the white community in which he lives:

In any other country in the world working for the BBC is something you wouldn't hesitate about and even be proud of, but here it's something you try not to mention in conversation. Most of the white community appear to be convinced that the difficulties of South Africa are entirely drummed up by people like me. One of the parents at the local school, who from a previous conversation appeared to be a reasonably intelligent well-informed lady, quite sincerely asked me if it really was an absolute requirement that I be a communist in order to join the BBC! And she really wasn't joking.

Such are the trials of BBC TV's only resident correspondent in Africa. Whilst stationed in South Africa, Michael Buerk played a key role in publicising the Ethiopian famine of 1984.

8 | Early Warnings: Ethiopia 1984

One of the most remarkable – and deeply depressing – features of the famine which struck Ethiopia in the early 1980s and killed over half a million people was the number of times the world was warned of an impending tragedy before it was finally roused by the images of Mohamed Amin and the commentary of Michael Buerk in October 1984. By the time that we in the west were eventually moved by television, it was long, long after the rains and harvests had failed repeatedly, and far too late to save the lives of the tens of thousands who had already died. Before looking at these early warnings in more detail, we need to examine briefly the background to this famine.

After the famine of 1973 and the revolution of the following year Ethiopia became embroiled in a whole succession of internal and external struggles which gravely sapped her energies. The new military rulers, the *Derg*, at first raised hopes that they might solve the difficult problem of rebellions in the provinces. They proclaimed the equality of all cultures and the right of minorities to some degree of local autonomy. For the first time Islam was granted official recognition and newspapers and radio were allowed to use languages other than the dominant Amharic.

Later, however, the *Derg* changed its tune and began to argue that since the old ruling class had been overthrown, there was no longer any justification for secessionist demands. It retreated to Haile Selassie's policy of armed confrontation with those it called 'bandits' and 'rebels'. So the war in Eritrea in the north dragged on. It is now Africa's longest-running war: the first shots had been fired in 1962. There were similar problems in Tigre in the north, in the Ogaden in the east and in the Oromo and Sidamo lands in the south. In fact, secessionist movements emerged at one time or another in 12 of Ethiopia's 14 provinces.

In the Ogaden, which is inhabited by Somali peoples, a full-blooded war broke out with neighbouring Somalia in 1977-8. Before 1977 Ethiopia had been armed by America and Somalia by Russia. When the Somalis invaded in July 1977, Ethiopia appealed to America for arms she had already ordered and paid for. The Americans, who had secretly encouraged the Somalis, declined to help a country which appeared to be going communist. The Ethiopians appealed, in desperation, to the Russians. For a time the bemused Russians armed both sides, then they withdrew from Somalia – to be replaced later by the Americans – and organised a massive airlift of supplies which saved the Ethiopian government from certain military defeat and probable political collapse. With the aid of 15,000 Cuban soldiers, Ethiopia launched a counter-attack in February 1978 and finally drove the Somalis out of the Ogaden. But guerrilla warfare continued to simmer and over a million refugees crossed the border into Somalia. The refugee problem throughout the country continued to mount and by the mid-1980s some 2 million Ethiopians from many regions had become refugees in Somalia, Djibouti and the Sudan.

Since the Ogaden War of 1977-8 defence expenditure in the region has escalated. Ethiopia now spends more per capita on military hardware than any other country in black Africa – a total of $378 million in 1981. Her army is now the second-best equipped on the continent, after South Africa's. For a decade half her budget has been spent on defence and vast manpower resources have been devoted to military struggles. Western critics make the obvious point that a poor country, and especially one so vulnerable to frequent drought, cannot 'afford' such luxuries. Jonathan Dimbleby, for example, argues that 'the mass mobilisation of peasantry, which began in 1975, to create a vast army of workers to go and fight in Eritrea and Tigre, was an appalling use of resources, if your fundamental problem is one of underdevelopment and poverty'.

At one level such criticicisms are self-evidently right, but ignore the fact that while Russia continues to pump arms into Ethiopia, America does the same in neighbouring Somalia, Sudan and Kenya. If Ethiopia scales down its arms buying unilaterally, it leaves itself vulnerable. So any agreement to spend less on arms needs to be made right across the Horn of Africa and to involve both super-powers if it is to have the remotest chance of being effective. The critics also often ignore the insanely high levels of defence expenditure in the west, in spite of the existence of escalating social problems. The fact remains, however, that much of Ethiopia's scarce resources are spent on military hardware that has no relevance to the daily lives of millions of impoverished peasants. This leaves little for investment in long-term economic development. The west, suspicious of the Ethiopian government's Marxism, has by and large chosen not to contribute to any such projects. Wars have also meant severe dislocation of peoples and farming activity and so have contributed directly to famines, with peasants who once sold a surplus now living at subsistence level. Both government and rebel troops are guilty of destroying food supplies, irrigation works and the like. At the height of the 1984-5 Ethiopian famine, it proved impossible to agree a safe passage arrangement, worked out by the United Nations, which would have allowed relief supplies to be moved from government-held to rebel-held parts of Eritrea and Tigre. The Ethiopian government was afraid that this would imply recognition of the rebels and might encourage dissidents elsewhere, while the rebels were also more interested in scoring political points than in relieving suffering. So thousands were left to die because they were unlucky enough to live in a political no man's land. Worse, there are authenticated stories of starving peasants being bombed, even napalmed, to death, which would seem, from the most cynical perspective, somewhat superfluous.

Added to war and dislocation as a major backdrop to famine is continuing environmental degradation. This is a complex subject, best simplified in the dramatic statistic that whilst a hundred years ago dense forests covered over 40 per cent of Ethiopia, today they cover less than 4 per cent, all in the south. This is the result of expanding cultivation, especially after the 1974 revolution, which gave peasants a real stake in the land for the first time. Trees have been cut recklessly for firewood and building houses. Deforestation has produced soil erosion, which in turn has made the country more vulnerable to drought. Very high densities of people and of livestock, especially in the north, have compounded the difficulties and contributed to the overworking and destruction of the soil. The country now loses an estimated 1.6 billion tonnes of topsoil annually through wind and water erosion, principally from the highland areas.

Confronted by such problems, the Ethiopian government has

maintained the policy, begun by Haile Selassie, of resettling people from the overcrowded north in the less populated south. It may
be an answer – many people believe it to be the only long-term
solution – and it was intensified in the wake of the 1984 famine.
But it has aroused fierce controversy, especially in the west, where
the question of how voluntary these movements of thousands of
people are, continues to be hotly debated. Some critics see the
whole thing as naked Stalinist brutality; others as a ploy to drive
away supporters of anti-government guerrillas; and yet others as
part of a long history of settling Amharic people in non-Amharic
lands. Whatever the reason, the west has largely washed its hands
of the scheme. So once again innocent people have paid the price
of other peoples' politics.

It is also very important when looking at the 1984 Ethiopian
famine to recognise that the drought which afflicted Ethiopia and
every other country in the Sahel in the early 1970s never really
went away, and so there was, at best, only a very partial recovery
from the disaster of 1973. There were years when conditions were
slightly more tolerable in some parts of the country, but basically
there was a prolonged drought throughout much of the south and
south-east from 1972 to 1980, which seriously undermined the entire way of life of the local cattle-keeping peoples. When conditions at last began to ease there in 1980, they started to get worse
in the north and continued to deteriorate year by year as the rains
failed and normally permanent rivers dried up. Areas which had
never before known serious drought began to be affected. The grip
of the drought tightened remorselessly to embrace 12 of the country's 14 provinces.

Local authorities, trying valiantly to cope, felt obliged to appeal
for outside help. People started to die in increasing numbers. By
February 1983, 1.3 million had walked into relief camps, while
many from Eritrea, hostile to the Ethiopian government, had fled
to the Sudan in a desperate search for food. By the end of 1984
almost 8 million people were suffering varying degrees of starvation. The seriousness of this long continuation of the drought was
obviously made even more acute by the man-made problems of
wars, refugees, resettlement and environmental destruction. One
set of problems merely reinforced the other.

There were many, many warnings of impending disaster. They
came from Ethiopian government officials; from United Nations

and relief agency workers; from missionaries; from newspaper, radio and television journalists, and even from photographers. They met with varying responses; some struck a chord, briefly, while others went unheeded. It is an unfortunate truism of famines that by the time the pictures are horrific enough to move people, it's almost too late. This may say something about the limitations of the media, or of our imaginations, or both.

An early example is the case of Anthony Suau, a 26-year-old staff photographer on the *Denver Post*. Suau came across a brief newspaper reference to Ethiopians suffering because of Cold War rivalries in the Horn of Africa. He asked his paper to send him out to investigate. The editor refused, saying: 'Ethiopia? Why would we want to go to Ethiopia? We just came back from Central America.' (*Popular Photography*, October 1984). So Suau went to his bank, drew out $5,000 he'd saved towards the cost of an apartment, and set off on unpaid leave. It was September 1983 and it was the first time he'd been outside America. He was stunned by the misery he saw – a year before Amin and Buerk. Suau returned with several rolls of horrific pictures. A few were published in the *Denver Post* and in a handful of dailies, but, as in 1973, the story was considered 'too downbeat' for American tastes and it 'died on the wire'. Many months later Suau was awarded a 1984 Pulitzer prize, which he donated to Catholic Relief Services in Ethiopia.

Then the Amin-Buerk story broke. Now at last Suau's pictures were in demand. As it became fashionable to be concerned, he was able to get out of debt. He said ruefully: 'Essentially I can eat because the Ethiopians can't'. The conclusion drawn by the magazine *American Photographer* is that 'for all its visual eloquence photography can no longer compete with television as a mass communicator.' Even if Suau's photographs had been published simultaneously in America's top ten newspapers, they could never have rivalled 'the initial slap in the face, the impact, exposure and immediacy of a two-minute video report on one of TV's national news programs'. (*American Photographer*, May 1985).

In Ethiopia itself, the Relief and Rehabilitation Commission (RRC) had been set up in 1974 in the wake of the earlier famine in an attempt to ensure that no Ethiopian government was caught as unprepared again by natural disaster as Haile Selassie's had been. One of its main functions is to operate an early warning system designed to alert the government and, if an approaching emergency is thought to be sufficiently severe, the world community. Over the years the RRC has earned the admiration, grudging at times, of most western governments, relief agencies and UN bodies. Many argue that it is the best organisation of its kind on the African continent. It was certainly very largely responsible for the fact that the severe drought in the south of the country in the late 1970s did not·lead to greater casualties. The RRC is a prime example of an African organisation grappling with an African problem, year in, year out, with scant resources, in a quite heroic way. People in the west hear very little about the work of the RRC, except if there is a dramatic story, as when its former Commissioner Dawit Wolde Giorgis left the country at the end of 1985 amid mutual recriminations.

Indeed, the images presented to us by the media tend to be only of westerners – Forsyth, Dimbleby, Buerk, Geldof and so on – saving Africa from disaster. To take just one example, when Peter Gill of Thames Television wanted to film famine in Karamoja, Uganda, in 1983 he was only able to do so by showing the arrival in the area of five pretty, white nurses. Much the same 'Angel of Mercy' approach was adopted by the British tabloids when the 1984 Ethiopian famine finally became a major story.

In the countdown to disaster in 1984, the RRC's warnings, its forecasts and its estimates of need were all chillingly accurate. The UN, however, had its own, highly-paid 'experts' on the spot. They reported differently, almost complacently. The world listened to the foreign experts. The world was wrong and Ethiopians died as a consequence. This shameful episode is fully documented in Peter Gill's excellent *A Year in the Death of Africa* (1986). As early as May 1981 the RRC had warned the UN that a serious creeping drought, brought about by repeated failure of the rains, was spreading remorselessly. Swift emergency action would be needed to alleviate future suffering.

Such warnings were repeated, frequently and urgently, throughout 1982 and 1983. Nobody paid much attention. In March 1984, by which time people were visibly pouring out of their villages into relief camps – always a danger sign – the RRC set up a meeting of all major government and donor agency representatives in Addis. It made a careful, dispassionate, well-researched appeal, which was repeated a few weeks later at the UN in New

York. It warned that a drought of unprecedented magnitude had hit the whole country, with several regions having had no rain for three consecutive years, and that, unless something was done immediately, millions of lives would be at risk and the death toll might rise 'to truly catastrophic proportions'.

This was duly picked up in the media, and there was some response from the public and a few pledges of aid, but the appeal was largely ignored by donor agencies. There were suspicions that the Ethiopians were 'crying wolf' once too often, despite the fact that famines can be averted only if people act in time. From March onwards the RRC made special efforts to take donor agencies to the worst affected areas to impress on them the need for urgency. Again to little effect.

In August, when none of the promised pledges of food had arrived. the RRC called another meeting of the international agencies. The warning was repeated with even greater urgency. Six million people were now affected. Ethiopians were contributing time, money and expertise to help the suffering, the RRC was setting up feeding and distribution stations but once again again there was apathy in the world outside. By now some Ethiopians were beginning to suspect that the west was playing politics and waiting for their Marxist government to be toppled by the famine, a view shared by many western relief and development workers. Reviewing the situation at the end of 1984, RRC Commissioner Dawit remarked:

> What makes us angry, and deeply sad at the same time, is that what is happening in many parts of the country now could so easily have been prevented. From the beginning of the year we predicted that, unless there was a massive inflow of grain, funds and other relief supplies, the situation would deteriorate appallingly . . . I cannot overemphasize the growing sense of shock that my staff and I felt when we realized that first our March appeal and then our August appeal had failed, when the days of indifference turned into the months of apathy, especially when we could see that – all around the country – our predictions were turning horribly true. An almost inconceivable nightmare was happening: Ethiopia was being forgotten by a world glutted with a surplus of grain; its humanitarian advocates had disappeared. (*The Challenges of Drought, RRC* 1985).

The western media was not guilty of ignoring the situation. Indeed, in the spring of 1983 BBC and ITN teams were taken on tours of northern Ethiopia and a joint appeal was launched, which brought in £2 million. At that time people were not dying in great numbers. A year later, in May 1984, two teams of about 25 journalists did the rounds. Earthscan, an environmental pressure group, took its team of African and European (largely Scandinavian) journalists around Ethiopia, while the UN High Commission for Refugees (UNHCR) took a rather more high-powered group around the Horn of Africa, including Somalia, Djibouti and Sudan, which included Mohamed Amin, and correspondents of *The New York Times*, *The Sunday Times*, Reuters, UPI and AFP. Lloyd Timberlake, Editorial Director of Earthscan and former science editor with Reuters, organised the former trip which led to his award-winning book, *Africa in Crisis* (1985). He remembers:

> We didn't know how bad it was in Ethiopia ourselves. We were going to look at soil erosion and desertification. Then we were going to take these journalists to Nairobi and show them what the UN had to say about soil erosion.

> We didn't see many people die, because it wasn't happening then, for peculiar reasons. But we certainly saw a lot of suffering and Korem was full – this was the time when the healthy people had made it into the camps. Just a few months later it was the people who had been starving for some time who came to the camps and died. Later we flew to Nairobi and realised how bankrupt the UN was in terms of ideas.

> I had earlier run across this UNHCR trip and they were telling *me* how bad it was. So at that time there were about 50 journalists and they were all writing horror stories.

Mohamed Amin wrote a story which appeared in the *Sunday Nation* of Kenya on 13 May under a half-page banner headline, 'Millions face death in Ethiopia.' Nobody paid much attention to the thousands of written words produced by these 50 newspaper journalists. A relief worker was solemnly told by a leading British newspaper that 'famine is not big news anymore'. This attitude persisted in Fleet Street. On 23 October, the day the famous Amin-Buerk film was first shown to the world, Chris Cramer, then BBC TV's Foreign News Editor, offered a full set of pictures to the *Sun*.

The response was: 'We're actually not interested in famine.' A few weeks later the *Sun* was sending its own reporters out to Ethiopia to get pictures.

In June Fr Mike Doheny and Paul Harrison went out to Ethiopia to make a film for the Irish charity Concern. Almost by chance, parts of it were shown on *Channel 4 News* and *News at Ten*. Fintan Farrelly, field director of Concern, had sent in Clare Chamberlain, a nurse and midwife from Dublin, to set up a feeding programme in Wolaita after hearing reports of severe malnutrition in what was considered to be a rich agricultural area. Concern had decided to focus its 1984 appeal on Ethiopia.

Originally, Fr Mike planned to go alone with his small 16mm Canon Scoopic camera with which he had made several fund-raising films in Africa and other parts of the world. Even in politically sensitive areas, few were prepared to stop a 70-year-old priest from filming. However, he fell off a London bus, injuring his hand, and independent film-maker Paul Harrison accompanied him on the trip. Harrison describes his initial impressions:

> As we drove south it began to look as if Fintan had exaggerated. The countryside around us was still green, and there were no obvious signs of drought or famine. All seemed well. There was poverty, as there is in most African rural areas, but no sign of starvation and death. Until we met Clare Chamberlain, the Dublin nurse who watched children die every day in her feeding centre. What she showed us took our complacency away.

The feeding centre was at Ado Bolosso. It consisted of a fenced-off compound within which was the local schoolhouse – a shed made of mud and sticks in the traditional fashion. In this building of 50 feet by 15 were about 400 wretched people, all of whom had made their way there from the surrounding countryside. Harrison recalls:

> The first impression was of the tremendous smell of humanity, like the warm smell of a cow shed, yet somehow different. The sounds were the coughs, cries, whines and moans of humans in various states of distress, disease, malnutrition and death. The sight was a wretched mass of destitution, human frames that barely contained lives, and had no fight left in them. There in the windowless gloom the inhabitants of the shelter looked like

they were being forced by starvation to pose for some awesome painting of the degradation of man.

We filmed in there, on the edge of the darkness that the camera would tolerate. I focused on the despairing faces looking half imploringly, half shamefully up at us. In the poor light, I filmed at half the normal speed to be sure of the exposure. Tears in my eyes made it hard to focus. They sat immobile. These were the humiliated failures, those who couldn't support their own families in food. Here widows lay in the dirt with their dying children, widowers sat as proudly as they could and waited their turn as the plastic cup of warm water and milk powder, which was the lunch for their children, came round. There was not enough food, money, personnel, medication, seeds or rain. It was a stupefying situation for a westerner to come across. We could hardly believe our eyes. We were just a week away from our normal world of throw-away plenty.

Mike and I felt physically weakened by what we saw. Numbly I aimed the camera at individual cases, at groups, at children and parents. I thought I was going to be sick. Clare indicated to me one small child lying listlessly on his mother's knee. I looked, wondering why she'd singled this one out for attention. Then I nearly passed out. An area of his leg was covered in flies. He had a hole in his leg like the hole that wasps make in an apple. A pink hole in his brown skin that was raw flesh, and the flies were just walking in and out of it. His worn-out mother paid no heed. I nearly threw up. I wasn't ready for this. I walked away. There was no point filming it. Nobody would ever show it. It was just too horrific. The child was being eaten at from the inside, his very flesh was being eaten away by flies.

Some distance away I turned the focus ring on the camera to 'macro' and walked back. I gritted my teeth and knelt down on the dirt beside him. I wanted to apologise to the mother as slowly I edged the camera into focus. I held my breath. As I filmed from a distance of six inches, flies flew in and out of the hole in his leg. They landed on my arms, my face. It was horrible.

Harrison and Fr Mike were both shattered by the experience, but the work was not finished yet. Harrison wanted to film a stand-up interview with Fr Mike at the door of the shelter. Fr Mike found

Father Mike Doheny with a child at the Ado Bolosso feeding station in Wolaita, June 1984. The film made there by Paul Harrison for the Irish charity Concern was one of the early warnings of the Ethiopian famine, and parts of it were shown on *Channel 4 News* and *News At Ten*.

himself on the spot. He had persuaded a reluctant Clare to be interviewed on film, telling her that it was quite simple; all she had to do was stand up and say what was in her heart. But then:

> Paul turned to me and said: 'You're next for interview, Mike.' I could have twisted his neck! But because I'd been preaching this thing, I couldn't say anything. So he stood me up and interviewed me, and I was in a state of severe shock. I'm not quite

sure what I said, but I certainly had no inhibitions at that particular moment.

When it was all over, I just sat down and said: 'Leave me alone.' And then the children came round and sat down on my knee. What they did to me I don't know, but they restored me, there's no doubt about that. They knew that I had tried to do something for them. It took me about 20 minutes to be able to move again and get on with the job. It was one of the most traumatic experiences that I've ever lived through.

Fr Mike flew straight back to Dublin and within a week those scenes from Ado Bolosso, horrific as they were, were shown on the evening news bulletin of RTE, Irish television. Within a fortnight Harrison had returned to London and they were then seen by an audience of millions on *Channel 4 News* and *News At Ten*. They were later seen in 12 countries. Then in August Paul arranged for Fr Mike and Clare to be interviewed on TV-am, though it nearly fell through at the last minute because of the breaking of the John de Lorean story. All this was impressive media coverage for what was originally conceived as a fund-raising film for Concern.

Television was generally far more interested and active than Fleet Street in the Ethiopian famine – unlike that of Biafra – and did its best to ring alarm bells. Chris Cramer of the BBC had a series of meetings with Oxfam and other aid organisations in the spring of 1984. Among the people he talked to was Paddy Coulter, Press Officer of Oxfam, who was acutely conscious that something was going seriously wrong in Ethiopia and wanted the media to be fully briefed. Chris Cramer says:

> I'd known Paddy for a while – he was a very good contact – and I wanted to explore with him the potential for doing a series of reports on famine. It was clear to us from earlier trips to Mozambique and to those parts of Zimbabwe that were suffering that there was obviously a famine story. Paddy agreed with me that there was clearly enough for a serious report.
>
> Although it's very difficult for me to sell the notion of a series of stories or features, I came to the conclusion that 1984 was going to be remembered as the year of the famine and that, like it or not, was clearly a very powerful journalistic argument to be doing stories.

Cramer was duly convinced by Coulter's evidence and he ran a series of famine-related pieces – by Mike Wooldridge on East Africa, on Chad as a spin-off from a piece about Libya's involvement in the civil war there, and on Upper Volta (now Burkina Faso) in the wake of Princess Anne's visit there for Save the Children. But Cramer was not satisfied with them 'because they weren't actually grasping the real problem.'

Things began to move in July, when the Disasters Emergency Committee (DEC) of the major British charities decided to launch a major famine appeal not just for Ethiopia, but for 11 African countries on the two television networks. Nothing like this had been attempted before.

The prime mover behind this appeal was Charles Stewart, a freelance film-maker. Stewart was in Ethiopia making a documentary for Central Independent Television on desertification. This was a long-term project, begun in the spring of 1983 and finally screened in mid-1985. It was based on one village and was called *Seeds of Hope*. Ironically, Stewart recalls: 'We particularly didn't want to do a disaster story; we wanted a story with some hope'.

The village in which Stewart filmed was on the border of Gondar and Wollo, in an area renowned for its good harvests. When Stewart first arrived it had endured three successive bad harvests. 1983 brought an unprecedented fourth. In January 1984 Stewart went in to Addis to try to find out whether the experience of 'his' village was typical of the country as a whole and whether an emergency appeal film should be made.

He had already established close contacts with the RRC, which had sent a team up to Wollo to investigate conditions there. Stewart was allowed to film the meeting at which this team reported back that 4.5 million people were not going to have enough food that year. This was the basis of the RRC's March appeal. Stewart remembers that:

> At that time hardly anybody thought there was a crisis. People would say that there'd been a crisis, with the exception of three years, for the last ten years. So it's an old crisis, just more of the same. Nobody quite appreciated that it was different. What made an enormous difference was the rains coming late again. In May it wasn't much worse than the year before, but as soon as the rains came late again it was definitely another disaster.

In our village, the caterpillar then came in and wiped out what remained. The instant that happened, the reaction amongst our farmers was: 'There are no rich and no poor anymore. We are now all dead'. They said: 'This is my death'. You thought it was just a saying, but they meant it quite literally.

Stewart found, however, that there were political objections to his making an appeal film:

I got no support at all, except from the RRC. A young Marxist country is very, very suspicious of the western media, because they believe they are done over by us, time and time again. By asking for a handout, the government is put in the position of losing its authority. It's no accident that Haile Selassie lost his authority totally after the '73 appeal, and I'm sure the present government was thinking about that at this time.

Anyway, I said to them that I thought a film should be made. They agreed but said that politically they didn't know whether I would be allowed to make it.

Stewart then flew back to London. On arrival he learned that Central TV agreed to support his idea of switching temporarily from the long-term *Seeds of Hope* to an emergency appeal, which was to be called *Seeds of Despair*. The RRC's Tafari Wossen came to London and agreed that the film could be made, on condition that 'you are not going to do us over'. Stewart went back in April, to Korem and along the famine road to Alamata, and shot the film, which tried to place the famine in context. Fr Mike, who was staying with Concern volunteers in Ibnat, recollects meeting Stewart who turned up at the opening of his tent one morning and invited himself to breakfast.

Back in London, whilst cutting his film, he showed it to the Disasters Emergency Committee, strongly urging it to launch an appeal for Ethiopia. The DEC was not at all keen, having made one in the recent past. Eventually it was persuaded to use Stewart's hour-long *Seeds of Depair* as the basis for its July appeal. But it stipulated that this was to be for 11 African countries affected by drought and not just for Ethiopia. The film was shown on all the independent networks at 10.30 pm on 17 July.

Meanwhile Chris Cramer at the BBC, knowing of ITV's plan to

use Stewart's documentary, decided to steal a march on them by using Michael Buerk, BBC TV's Southern African Correspondent. Buerk had been posted to Johannesburg in 1983. He had worked first in newspapers, including the *Daily Mail*, and local radio before moving to BBC TV, where he worked as a reporter and then as industrial correspondent, a role he quickly abandoned. He was recruited by Alastair Hetherington for BBC Scotland, but later returned to London as special correspondent and covered the Falklands War from Argentina. With some reluctance he read the *Nine o'clock News* for a year and a half. Buerk had always wanted to be a foreign correspondent and to live abroad with his family. He had tried for Washington, but was turned down, and so jumped at the offer of Johannesburg.

Even his rivals are quick to acknowledge Buerk's abilities. Peter Gill of Thames comments that 'no one would doubt that Mike Buerk is absolutely first rate when it comes to putting evocative commentaries over pictures, as he does so brilliantly from South Africa', while Chris Cramer, his boss at the time, believes 'the man is one of the best television correspondents in the world. He's an amazing writer and one of the few people who knows how to blend pictures with words.'

In July 1984 Buerk received a call from the BBC's Foreign Desk in London, asking him to do a story for the joint famine appeal:

> The BBC producer, who was helping to put together the five-minute BBC appeal, wanted a reporter or correspondent to place himself in some area where famine was a particular problem and deliver some faintly spurious authenticity – to say: 'Now today in so-and-so'. This request had come in ridiculously late. It was a week before the thing was going out. Where would I like to go? And while I was there, could I do a news report as well? Loony! The place I wanted to go was Mozambique. But the logistics of trying to get into northern Mozambique and out again on the time scale were just impossible.

In 'quiet desperation' Buerk cabled his friend Paddy Coulter of Oxfam. Despite the obvious obstacles and the fact that the likely cost 'would presumably keep Upper Volta in asparagus for years', Buerk was keen to go, seeing it as 'an opportunity to do some good, if only it can be managed'. Coulter suggested Ethiopia, where he knew that things were getting desperate, and where both he and Mohamed Amin, Visnews' Bureau Chief for Africa, had excellent contacts. Amin was not able to film with Buerk on this occasion, as he was already committed to working on safari with the film star Brooke Shields as part of a series, *Lifestyles of the Rich and Famous*. But he organised an alternative crew, under his colleague Mohinder Dhillon, and the necessary travel documents, while Oxfam took care of the visas. Buerk was to go to Wolaita, where Oxfam was operational and where Fr Mike and Harrison had recently filmed. Buerk explains:

> Oxfam said that there was a problem occurring in the southern part of the country, an area that was not normally afflicted with a shortage of rainfall, but had been, and the effects were really quite interesting, because although it wasn't anything like as bad as it was in the north, the people were culturally not as prepared to deal with that sort of situation. And that because there weren't the same military sensibilities about the south of the country as there were about the north, we might just be able to get in there and out again.
>
> So we did. We filmed these people starving and dying in these huts in the pouring rain – it was one of those awful paradoxes. It made quite an impression on me, though it paled obviously in the light of what happened later. We actually had about eight hours there in the end to go down and get back. We flew back to Nairobi and satellited it from there and it actually got to London in time by some miracle. There was a bit of our film in the appeal and a bit in the news and it raised quite a lot of money.

The BBC appeal went out on 17 July a few hours before *Seeds of Despair*. Two days later the DEC's appeal for the 11 African countries was launched by Frank Bough on BBC TV, Joanna Lumley on ITV and Sue MacGregor on BBC Radio. On 23 July extracts from the Doheny-Harrison film were shown on *Channel 4 News* and ITN's *News At Ten*, and served to reinforce the main appeals. These appeals of July 1984 were phenomenally successful in pre-Geldof figures, with almost £10 million pouring into the DEC during the next three months. But just as the Committee was about to close its books and congratulate itself on a job well done, Amin,

Buerk and Peter Gill made new films which forced it, not without some reluctance, to keep its books open, wide open.

On the eve of disaster Peter Cutler and Rob Stephenson of the International Disaster Institute (now the Relief and Development Institute) went to Ethiopia to look at the state of food emergency preparedness there. They found the situation truly desperate. Peter Gill quotes Cutler as saying:

> I remember coming back in September 1984 and literally giving up. We were just banging our heads against a brick wall. I'd tried all the donor agencies and the media. People were sick of my going on and on about it. Then along came BBC Television and everything changed overnight. (*A Year in the Death of Africa*).

Rob Stephenson's recollection is equally graphic:

> The most interesting experience of my life and the most powerful was actually being in Ethiopia three weeks before it crashed. It's hard to describe what it feels like to sit somewhere and just know that there are going to be 2 million people on the road in two weeks. It's an extraordinary sensation. You were watching a whole society just about to collapse.

At this precise moment the Ethiopian government was celebrating the tenth anniversary of the overthrow of Haile Selassie.

9 | Filming Famine: October 1984

The harvesting of news stories is always an extremely unpredictable business. In 1973 a chain of coincidence led Jonathan Dimbleby to make a film which exposed 'the unknown famine' to the world, and which also played a key role in the revolution that brought down Haile Selassie. In October 1984 a Visnews film shot by Mohamed Amin, narrated by Michael Buerk, shown first on BBC TV News and then around the world, provoked an unprecedented response which culminated in the global Live Aid pop concert and Sport Aid's Race Against Time. Millions of pounds were raised by ordinary men, women and children throughout the world to help the famine victims of Ethiopia. It was one of the biggest media stories ever to come out of Africa.

There are many misconceptions surrounding the Amin-Buerk film. There is a theory, first put out by *The Sunday Times*, and subsequently repeated on many occasions, that the whole thing was a complete accident – that a BBC crew, changing planes in Addis Ababa, somehow stumbled across the famine by accident. It is a nice story, but totally untrue. It is also widely believed that Michael Buerk was the first to go into Ethiopia to film after the independence celebrations and that the whole affair was a BBC operation. This too is incorrect; the story is much more complex and more interesting than that.

After the impact of the July appeals, there were a number of media people wanting to get back into Ethiopia as soon as possible to publicise what they and Oxfam felt might become an even greater disaster story. They included Mohamed Amin of Visnews and Mike Wooldridge of BBC Radio, both of whom were based in neighbouring Kenya. In London there was Peter Gill, a reporter with Thames Television's current affairs programme *TV Eye*, while in Johannesburg Michael Buerk was also anxious to return. Not all of them were aware of the interest of their rivals, but they were all in touch with Oxfam and other charities and tried, in a variety of ways, to extract travel visas from the Ethiopian authorities.

But throughout August and September the Ethiopians were issuing no visas to foreign reporters to cover the famine. Journalists were welcome to report the tenth anniversary celebrations, but they were not allowed to travel outside Addis. Similar restrictions applied to aid agency officials based in the capital. In September Mike Wooldridge went in and tried to arm-twist his way out of Addis, but without success. He was told to return later if he wanted to cover the famine.

The total cost of the celebrations, organised by the North Koreans, was estimated at $200 million by the Americans. That is certainly an exaggeration fuelled by political distaste; they were not so publicly critical of the extravagance of leaders they supported, like Marcos or Duvalier. Peter Gill provides a description of the celebrations in the opening chapter of *A Year in the Death of Africa*. Every government department was told to spend part of its budget improving its office buildings; roads in Addis were newly tarred; beggars were rounded up and sent packing; out-of-town roadblocks kept desperate peasants out of the capital, as they had done in 1973; Ethiopian Airlines became the first in Africa to order the Boeing 767, buying two at $60 million each; Crow of Reading won a £3 million contract to improve television coverage for the celebrations; a plush new Congress Hall was built by the Finns; there was an alleged consignment of half a million bottles of whisky to replace those already drunk. And so the list went on.

There is no doubt that the government squandered money, as Haile Selassie had done a decade earlier when hosting the tenth anniversary of the founding of the Organisation of African Unity. But western critics who were so quick to berate Marxist Ethiopia were often extremely slow to criticise corruption in pro-western countries such as Sudan. Celebrations of this kind tend to fulfil an important symbolic role in most newly independent countries – both pro- and anti-western – in a way not always appreciated by western journalists.

What was important in Ethiopia was the fact that the celebrations distracted attention and manpower away from the famine at a crucial moment. For the four weeks prior to the celebrations, for example, officials of the Relief and Rehabilitation Commission

(RRC) were, according to Peter Cutler and Rob Stephenson, 'involved for the majority of their time in practising various parade and banner-waving exercises'. This was viewed 'with some disquiet' by both local and foreign relief workers. Even more important was the fact that, yet again, the rains failed. Ethiopia normally has two rainy seasons: *belg* (from February to May) and *meher* (from June to September). In 1984 the *belg* rains failed completely. All hope then rested on the *meher* rains. But these were late to start – in some areas they didn't start at all – and they finished a month earlier than usual, leaving millions facing starvation. With an irony comparable to Michael Buerk's launching a famine appeal in the rain in July, towards the end of the revolutionary celebrations on 12 September there was another brief torrential downpour.

Just 48 hours earlier, Oxfam had issued a press release. It was headed: 'Ethiopian famine; will Oxfam's largest ever grant shame western governments into immediate action?' It pointed out that the vast grain stocks accumulating in the EEC were not available for emergency use and that since some 6 million people were now at risk in Ethiopia, Oxfam had decided, in a major break with past policy, to buy 10,000 tonnes of grain itself and ship it out to Ethiopia immediately. It hoped by this gesture 'to galvanise Western governments into sending urgent grain supplies to Ethiopia'.

One person who was galvanised was Peter Gill of Thames Television. Gill was a journalist with a deep understanding and long experience of Africa, dating back to his time with VSO in the Sudan in 1966-7. He was fully aware that it had taken great courage on the part of individuals at Oxfam to have been publicly rude about the EEC and the British government. Gill waved this press release, which he thought 'an extraordinarily effective way of presenting the story', in front of his editor and was immediately given the go-ahead to make a *TV Eye* documentary about Ethiopia. It was to be called *Bitter Harvest*. Gill harked back to Jonathan Dimbleby's 1973 film, which he found 'extraordinary, appalling and very nearly unwatchable' but without any political message. This, as we have seen, was a conscious decision on Dimbleby's part. But as Gill points out:

> When it came to our making the film and my wanting to respond to the Ethiopian situation, we had to find an additional element. What prompted us to move as film makers was the direct

comparison with European grain surpluses and the fact that Oxfam in September were making a particular issue of that, and put out a press release saying that the British government, the EEC and others were behaving disgracefully because they were not prepared to contribute any part of their surpluses to Ethiopia. It was that and, if you like, anti-Common Market prejudices, and our capacity to link the two that enabled us to do the film.

Gill joined the queue of media people pounding away at the Ethiopians for visas. He has since argued that such rivalry and competition between the networks was good for the exposure of the Ethiopian famine. Gill's project gained the support of Hugh Goyder, Oxfam's Field Director in Ethiopia, and, crucially, of the RRC, which liked his political approach and the idea of contrasting Europe's plenty with Ethiopia's poverty. It preferred this to the BBC's proposed orthodox news coverage, which would concentrate on the horror and leave it at that. As it happens, Gill was not alone in his approach:

> Before we even went out, BBC's Sunday night *Heart of the Matter* did precisely our story. They had a smaller budget, they used a bit of library film, they didn't have all the latest details and they stood Oxfam people up in corn fields, but they were on precisely the same tack.

Because the Ethiopian government supported his political message, Gill was the first journalist to receive a visa to look at the famine after the anniversary celebrations. The visas took about three weeks to come through and were initially specified only for Wolaita in the south, where Buerk, Fr Mike and Harrison had been in July. Both the RRC and Oxfam advised Gill not to reckon on going to the north – where the famine was more severe and where guerrilla movements were active – but to concentrate on Oxfam projects in the south, to mention 'drought' rather than 'famine' and so on. So Gill flew out to Addis. At the RRC's office he had the satisfaction of hearing Mike Wooldridge of the BBC phoning from Nairobi almost every hour asking: 'Where are these visas?'

He started filming in Wolaita, but on 3 October a meeting of the Ethiopian Politburo at last officially gave priority to 'the drought' and agreed to let journalists travel north. Since Gill was already in the country, he went to Korem on 8 October, the first journalist to do so in several months. It was the epicentre of the famine. Tens of thousands were gathered there. Scores were dying every day. He found that he could 'just about cope with the dead and the dying. It was the despair of the living that finally put paid to my sense of detachment.'

Gill finished shooting his film. Shortly before he flew back to England, he was amazed to find his advice being sought by the authorities:

> We were being asked, if you please, when the BBC news team should be let in! This was because the Ethiopians really were anxious that our more political approach should be shown first, especially as we were knocking the targets that they had in mind, whereas, rightly or wrongly, the BBC didn't have targets in mind, they simply had an extraordinary story. That's their role and ours, as a documentary team, is slightly more elaborate.

Ironically, both the Ethiopian authorities and Gill were to be disappointed, for he flew home to be confronted by a technicians' dispute at ITV. His film would not be shown! Oxfam and Save the Children appealed on humanitarian grounds for 'this powerful film' to be screened as a 'special case'. Thames tried to show it on a management-run local service, but the union continued to black it. Only when the details were reported in the press was there a change of heart. By then Amin and Buerk had gone out to Ethiopia, shot their film and had pipped Thames to the post by 48 hours! Everyone now remembers the Amin and Buerk film. Gill's role is largely forgotten as is that of the broadcaster Mike Wooldridge, who accompanied Amin and Buerk and filed a number of powerful radio reports. Such are the quirks of media fortune.

The second post-celebrations visa went not to the BBC, but to Mohamed Amin, Africa Bureau Chief of Visnews. Amin is a Kenyan, the son of a poor railway worker, and a cameraman of international reputation with many years' experience of filming in Africa and throughout the world. His major exclusives had included the Zanzibar Revolution, the assassination of Tom Mboya, the abortive 1982 coup in Kenya, and the finding of Idi Amin after his overthrow, though the credit for that was claimed by the BBC's Brian Barron. Amin has numerous personal contacts in Ethiopia, was adept at dealing with the notoriously difficult bureaucracy and was able to move in and out in a way that western journalists could not match.

Though the low-profile Visnews and the BBC are allies, the creative tension that exists between the two was to be important in the developments that followed. What needs to be stressed is that both Visnews and the BBC were chasing the Ethiopian famine story independently and they were only to come together almost by accident and at the last minute. Kevin Hamilton, Managing Editor of Visnews in London, points out that Visnews had already twice been to Ethiopia, in May and July:

> We couldn't get permission to go to the areas that we knew were very badly affected. Mo Amin has a great deal of autonomy and we rely very heavily on his feedback to us. We'd sat here and discussed the Ethiopian situation often. When he first started saying: 'This famine is not just another African famine', we said to him: 'Come back to us with all the information you can get, and when the time is right, budget constraints permitting, we'll go in'.

> Mo eventually called Brendan Farrow, our News Coverage Manager, and said: 'The crucial thing is whether the next rains fail, and they must come within a week or two'. And when they did fail, that was the point at which he said to us: 'I'm going', and we agreed.

Amin's recollection of these events is that:

> We made several attempts to get permission to go to northern Ethiopia during the course of the year, but none was forthcoming. Finally, in mid-October I was in London for a meeting with Visnews and impressed on them that we should certainly look at the famine in Ethiopia again. It was then agreed that I should go in as quickly as possible and that we should increase the pressure to get permission and go immediately. I phoned the RRC and Ministry of Information from London to seek permission. I flew back to Nairobi arriving on Sunday 14 October and I came straight to the office to prepare our equipment for the flight on Monday morning to Addis.

Though Visnews normally supplies unvoiced film to its customers, Kevin Hamilton on this occasion was keen for BBC Radio's Mike Wooldridge to join Amin's team, for he was aware that pictures on their own, however good, often fail to make the maximum impact. He was afraid that without the presence of a correspondent who knew the area and the story well, Amin's film might get some half-baked commentary pasted onto it in London. In the event, and at the very last minute, it was Michael Buerk, rather than Mike Wooldridge, who was to supply the commentary. Mohamed Amin explains how this came about:

> At that point I was going with my sound man Zik Njuguna. Also coming with me was the BBC Radio correspondent, Mike Wooldridge, who is based in Nairobi. We very often work together. But as far as television coverage was concerned it was absolutely an exclusive Visnews assignment. Mike was coming along to do his radio piece and he might well have done an interview or a camera piece for BBC TV News.
>
> During the course of that Sunday, I got a call from Michael Buerk in Johannesburg asking if he could come along. I explained to him the problems of the travel permits, the permission, and the visas, and told him that I thought it would be very difficult for him to come. He understood and that was the end of the conversation as far as I was concerned. But obviously he talked to the BBC in London. He called me back again a couple of hours later and put a bit of pressure on me to try and help him, and I agreed. I told him that I would call the head of the RRC's information division, Tafari Wossen, who has been a friend of mine for the past 20 years, at his house.
>
> Wossen's immediate reaction was very negative because having done so much work to get the permits he could not now easily change them. But after a bit of pressure he agreed to do what he could the next day, Monday 15th, provided that we delayed our trip for a couple of days. So I agreed that we should go on Wednesday 17 October instead in order to try and get permission for Michael Buerk to come with us. In fact, after I told London we were delaying our trip by 48 hours there was a very strong reaction from the newsroom there and I was told: 'OK, we agree to your going on Wednesday'. But if there was any more delay because of Michael Buerk then we must go in on our own, as indeed had been the plan all along.
>
> Finally we were told that Michael Buerk would be issued a visa and they would try to process his permits by the time we got there on Wednesday. I gave this news to Mike, so he flew up

from Johannesburg on 16 October, arriving in Nairobi late that night, and joined us the next morning on the 17th.

Since his earlier visit for the July appeal, Michael Buerk had been in frequent contact with Paddy Coulter of Oxfam and had thus kept in touch with developments in Ethiopia – not an easy thing to do from South Africa. This explains why, when he heard that Mohamed Amin had got visas, he was so keen to climb aboard, and Buerk readily admits that without Amin's help he would never have made the trip.

So on 17 October, Amin, Buerk, Wooldridge and Njuguna, the sound man, flew from Nairobi to Addis, five days after Peter Gill had left. They checked in with the RRC and into the Hilton and then spent two days arguing with the Ethiopians about visas. Amin recalls that:

> The permits that we were given were not for the areas that we had asked for. It's a complex story but it involved long discussions and rather angry exchanges with officials of the RRC and Ministry of Information. We felt we had been misled by them telling us that we were going to Makelle and Korem but now we were being told we were going somewhere else. Eventually, after a few rows, we got the travel permits to go to Makelle, Lalibela and Korem, which were the three most seriously affected areas and where journalists were not allowed. In fact, no foreign journalist had been allowed into Makelle since the revolution ten years before.

Amin and Wooldridge had planned to go to Korem all along. They had been before and knew the scale of the disaster there. Michael Buerk explains:

> It was the furthest place you could get to up the spinal road from Addis. You could not drive north of Korem because of the civil war that was going on. So that tended to be the place where the relief agencies could best get food into, and therefore it became a catchment area for refugees. It was on the border of the accessible area and the inaccessible area, and people knew that and came clustering in to get the food.

The decision to go to Makelle in the heart of Tigre Province, where a civil war raged and where, as Amin says, no foreign journalist had been allowed for the past decade, was conditioned by two factors. First, Peter Gill's Thames crew had also been to Korem, but no further north, and Amin and Buerk were therefore under competitive pressure to go further and get better material. Amin and Wooldridge had heard from various sources that things were far worse there than at Korem, and this they later confirmed – no food had been able to reach the beleaguered town for two weeks because of rebel activity. Second, they had got hold of a plane, which was the only way to get into Makelle. As for Lalibela, the holy place which Bob Geldof later visited, that was nearly, as Amin recounts, a costly mistake:

> Our initial flight plan was to stop in Lalibela and then go into Makelle. However, we decided while in mid-air to overfly Lalibela and go on to Makelle, returning to Lalibela on the way back. The reason for this was that we had been there before and did not want to take any chances in case the bureaucracy got into the act and gave us more problems. As it happened, in fact, at about exactly the same time Lalibela was being taken over by the Tigrean rebels. Had we landed, God only knows what would have happened. We would probably have been arrested and could have spent several months with the rebels before being released in the Sudan.

They spent the night of Friday 19th in Makelle, flew on to Alamata on the Saturday, from where they drove to Korem, spending the night there, then they flew back to Addis on the Sunday and left Ethiopia on Monday 22 October.

This brief trip proved as traumatic for these seasoned and supposedly hardened newsmen as the impact which Amin's film was soon to provoke around the world. Michael Buerk describes the effect on them:

> We drove through the 'town' of Makelle, and there was this sort of bank which went down, slightly wooded, little bit of a church, and there were something like 50,000 people there. It was quite extraordinary. The curious thing – it came out in the first film that we did – is the biblical business. People looked like those depicted in the colour illustrations in my old school Bible. Sort of sackcloth colour and a certain nobility of features. I think it's a factor that the Ethiopians' distress did engage people's sym-

pathy precisely because they're such a fine-looking people. I know it's silly, but it's a natural reaction.

Then we went down to this place where they had these huge sheds and went in and everybody was just dying in front of us. There was a sepulchral feeling about the whole place. People were just in there dying. There was a feeling of total apathy and helplessness, and there wasn't anything very much that anybody seemed to be able to do about it all. There they were, packed into sheds. A few people crying. People dying.

The curious thing was that I'd been in the job for quite a long time and one tends to have quite a detached and professional attitude about it. I sometimes think to myself, particularly in South Africa, 'bloody hell, this is a good story, somebody's been burned to death!' You feel this dreadful divergence between 'gosh, this is a really good story' and 'Christ, this is absolutely tragic'. But I didn't feel that about Ethiopia at all. In fact I got quite overwhelmed, and so did Mohamed Amin, whose experience of this sort of thing was much greater than mine.

It sounds trite to say it, but the whole thing seemed so absolutely ghastly that we had to be jogged into actually doing something about it at times. A little later on, in Korem, we didn't even speak to each other. Mo just went through the motions of filming these people when they were dragging the bodies out in the morning and none of us, Mo or Mike or myself, actually passed a word for about two hours. We went through the motions of doing the coverage and asking the questions of people from time to time, but we felt quite different to how one normally does in covering an ordinary story.

Amin confirms this sense of deep shock. Even with all his experience and local knowledge, he confesses he had 'absolutely no idea of the scale of the disaster.' The actual filming itself was also fraught – at least for Buerk. Amin was using an early model Betacam camera. Normal ENG camera batteries are heavy, bulky things, but the Betacam used slim, light ones, which had a very short life of about three minutes. It was impossible to recharge them, since the electricity at Korem was sporadic and in any event not of sufficiently high voltage. Amin had only brought about 15 batteries, and Buerk was 'in a panic, absolutely terrified' that they would run out before they'd finished filming.

Mohamed Amin filming in Ethiopia during his trip with Michael Buerk.

While they were still in Ethiopia, Mike Wooldridge filed a strong radio report, but it did not receive the necessary support in London and was not given peaktime exposure. But even if it had been, there is no way that a radio report, however skilled the correspondent, could have carried the impact of Buerk's commentary combined with Amin's camerawork. The latter, in Peter Gill's view, was 'truly exceptional':

> It is actually the cameraman who has got to get in among some not only very distressing, but also very worrying situations of people who are desperately ill and probably desperately diseased as well. And Mohamed Amin was right in amongst them and that was part of the appeal of that footage, while Buerk's commentary was truly memorable.

They all flew back to Nairobi on the Monday. Buerk had already arranged for an editor to fly up from Johannesburg. They assembled at Amin's studio and sat down to edit the first of the two films they were to make. It was an uncomfortable task, as Amin recalls:

> While we were editing the material, looking at it over and over again, everybody in the room broke down and cried. It was just totally unbelievable what had been going on.

At this point Buerk called London and spoke to his boss, Chris Cramer. He was still 'a bit knocked sideways' and not altogether coherent, but managed to convey that the footage Amin had shot was quite out of the ordinary. The original plan had been to satellite all the material from Nairobi, since it was not possible to do this from Addis. However, Cramer now decided that Buerk should bring the film to London himself on the overnight plane, 'rather than screw around with satellites'. Cramer explains why he took this unusual decision:

> If you believe you've got four or five minutes' worth of programme material out of a total 20 minutes of film, getting that across by satellite is terribly expensive. If we'd satellited it all from Nairobi, the total cost would have been £5-6,000. Bringing Mike to London meant that he could sit down with people who are editing the programmes here, and they could discuss what they want to put out. A tired correspondent is often not the best judge of what a story's worth. Foreign and domestic correspondents are used to cutting two-minute packages for news; they're not used to cutting eight- or ten-minute ones. Mike

knew that he had a wealth of awful material and I felt that we could handle it better if he was here. It was also cheaper to fly him here and he could get a decent night's sleep on the plane and come in completely fresh. When you know you've got a huge international story, it's much easier to do it that way.

So, in the reporting of such a significant story, satellite technology was bypassed.

Alas for Buerk's 'decent night's sleep on the plane'! Tired as he was, Michael Buerk decided that there was still work to be done:

The editor I'd taken up from Johannesburg cut the picture for the first piece, eight minutes long, and we just managed to do that in time. I climbed onto the plane with all the rushes and with the first film and wrote the script all through the night on the plane, which I think in retrospect was probably quite a useful exercise, because I was isolated on the plane with everything still fresh in my mind. I was probably better able to distil the feelings that I'd got from being there that way than any other.

I got to London in the morning and the first film was shown that lunchtime, which was a helluva scramble. And what was even more of a scramble, I wrote and voiced the commentary for the second film, which lasted seven minutes, in two hours the next morning. And it went out that day.

The commentary that he wrote on the plane, which went with the first film, began:

Dawn, and as the sun breaks through the piercing chill of night on the plain outside Korem, it lights up a biblical famine, now, in the 20th century. This place, say workers here, is the closest thing to hell on earth. Thousands of wasted people are coming here for help. Many find only death. They flood in every day from villages hundreds of miles away, felled by hunger, driven beyond the point of desperation. Death is all around. A child or an adult dies every 20 minutes. Korem, an insignificant town, has become a place of grief.

This film, presenting without restraint the sight and sounds of death in a 'biblical famine', moved to tears first hardened television newsrooms and then audiences all around the world. And then, in a rare display of powerful popular pressure, people began demanding that their governments do something.

10 | Reactions: 1984 – 86

When Michael Buerk arrived in London on the morning of Tuesday 23 October, he first delivered a copy of the rushes to Visnews, since it was their film. While he went off to Television Centre at Wood Lane to write and voice the second film, Visnews editors at Park Royal put together a five-minute package (compared to the normal 90-second item), which was sent out around the world as part of their daily satellite transmissions. This was unvoiced and – as if to underline Kevin Hamilton's fear that pictures alone often don't make the impact they should – Eurovision promptly turned it down, despite a note telling them to take special note of this extraordinary material. The Belgian television official in charge of co-ordinating at the time has often been reminded of this decision.

He was not alone, however. When it came to getting the film shown in America on NBC, with which Visnews and the BBC have close links, there was initially a similar reluctance and the film needed some definite pushing. America, traditionally, has not been an easy market for African famine stories – Jonathan Dimbleby's 1973 film was never screened and Anthony Suau's 1983 photos were ignored. It looked at first as though history was going to repeat itself.

Visnews executives saw the first BBC showing, on the midday news, and were highly impressed by Buerk's commentary. Kevin Hamilton immediately phoned Joe Angotti, then European Manager of NBC News, to ask if he had seen the BBC News. He said he hadn't, so Hamilton told him that he must get hold of it right away and have a look at it. Angotti did so, immediately agreed that it was exceptional material and called New York. New York at first didn't want to know; the Line-up Editor was not interested. Angotti continued to push. While he was doing so, Frieda Morris, NBC's Bureau News Chief in London, alerted by the BBC's Chris Cramer, had seen the BBC news item. She too rang New York and urged NBC to take 'this amazing piece of television'. She got the same response; there was some far more important domestic crisis.

Eventually NBC reluctantly agreed to accept a special satellite, booked ahead of the normal time. According to Chris Cramer, Morris was told to get it revoiced by an American correspondent. She refused. They said they didn't want 'a goddamn English voice'. She told them: 'I will send this to you and you will run it, I guarantee it'.

She was right. They did run it though not at full length, with Buerk's English voice, which was extraordinary for NBC. When the film arrived, the whole of the NBC newsroom sat in silence watching it, totally stunned. Tom Brokaw, the presenter, said: 'Right, clear the decks, we're going to run this'. They ran it with a humble introduction, saying: 'We do these major political stories from time to time, but there are certain types of story we never bring you. This is one. Here is a BBC News report by Michael Buerk'.

The first film, from Korem, all eight minutes of it, also profoundly moved the staff at the BBC TV newsroom; Chris Cramer had never seen so many so-called cynics cracking up. For him, it was one of those exceptionally rare moments in television history. Afterwards he wished he'd had the foresight to record it. Later, people in the newsroom 'put their hands in their pockets and come out with 200 quid, which is quite unheard of'.

The film was initially shown on BBC's midday news. It went out as the first item. This pattern was repeated on the *Six o'clock News*. But, because there is a good deal of rivalry between the *Six o'clock News* and the *Nine o'clock News*, the editor decided to be different. He ran it as the fourth story, behind some trivial development in the miners' strike and two other items. The next day there was a headline in the *Daily Mail*: 'The pictures that shattered the conscience of the world.' At the BBC, Michael Buerk scribbled on a copy: 'And that ran as the fourth story on the *Nine o'clock News*!'

It provoked some bad feeling at the time that Mohamed Amin's camerawork was at first not credited. It was after all his film, a Visnews film, which Buerk had brought to London. The BBC were fully entitled to show it, but it was not their film. The issue centred around union rules regarding the use of non-BBC camera crews. Financial constraints at the BBC had meant a cutback on the number of trips made by London-based camera crews. It was getting more and more expensive to send two- or three-man crews out with all the excess baggage and overtime entailed. So it became increasingly usual for BBC correspondents sent abroad to use Visnews, freelance or – occasionally – NBC cameramen. This created a morale problem with television crews in London and it was something about which the union felt very strongly. An agreement was reached whereby BBC correspondents going abroad could use other crews only for a one-day shoot. Anything more, as now in the case of Amin and Buerk, had to be cleared first with the union.

Because of the speed with which this operation had been mounted, and because Buerk had locked into a Visnews-planned operation at the last minute, the union's agreement had not been sought. There were fears, as with Peter Gill's film at Thames, that Amin's film might be 'blacked'. Chris Cramer explained the situation to the union, stressing in particular that they could never have got visas for a BBC crew in time, and the union agreed to drop its objections – but at a price.

The price was that Amin's camerawork would not be credited on the news, and neither would the fact that the film originated from Visnews. Cramer accepts that, with hindsight, he was probably over-reacting to these in-house difficulties. And, indeed, when the second report went out, on 24 October, Amin was credited. The journalists at the BBC, who were as excited about the pictures as the Visnews editors, were strongly in favour of giving Amin an on-air credit. But the BBC cameramen didn't want salt rubbed into their wounds by the praising of a non-BBC cameraman for his part in the operation. This original problem was later compounded on the Wednesday when, after a change of shift at the BBC newsroom, the new editors and writers came in, found no reference at all to Amin, assumed they were BBC pictures, and began reporting this to the world. As Tim Arlott, News Editor of Visnews, puts it:

> When it's the cameramen's work, and they go out and they work their butts off, it's one thing not to get a credit, but it's quite another when their material is credited to someone else!

Visnews was even more aggrieved when BBC Enterprises began offering Amin's films for sale, and decidedly not amused when within 48 hours the United States Information Agency rang them up to say: 'You'll never believe it, we've got these fantastic pictures from Ethiopia. Would you like to buy them?' Kevin Hamilton concludes that:

> Maybe we were a little bit lax in our efforts to publicise our own role, but we didn't want to upset the BBC. We didn't want to rub it in the face of the unions at the BBC. Under normal circumstances, had it not been for this ban, Mo would have got an immediate credit on the BBC and it wouldn't have become a problem.

In the long run Amin did receive the recognition that was his due and went on, in Buerk's words, to 'do amazing things' and enhance his reputation, notably with his stunning half-hour documentary film *African Calvary*. Michael Buerk, reflecting back on this period, comments:

> There was an element of angst between the BBC and Visnews, as there always is in this sort of thing. If you're an agency with this wonderful 'once in a decade' thing that your cameraman has actually filmed, you are fairly anxious to make sure that people know that 'this is Visnews'. I think it all worked out in the end and fortunately didn't create any sort of problems between me and Mo, which is really all that concerned me.

Immediately after the Amin-Buerk films were shown, the phones started ringing all around the world. To take just one example. Djibril Diallo, of the United Nations Development Programme, had been in Ethiopia that month. He had woken in a camp one morning to find himself in the midst of the bodies of 30 people who had died in the night. He had also had a young girl die in his arms after her desperate mother had implored him to take her with him – an image, he says, that will stay with him forever. Diallo writes that:

> It was this horror, this trauma, which was brought under control in part thanks to the media's influence. Anyone who doubts the power of television should have been in my New York office immediately after the screening of the now famous BBC News film. My telephone lines were jammed by calls from people in tears saying they had not known it was as bad as this and offering their help. (*African Reflections on a Famine*, 1985).

On 25 October, the day after the second Amin-Buerk film was shown on BBC News, the technicians at Thames at last relented and Peter Gill's political documentary, *Bitter Harvest*, was finally screened. Gill is remarkably philosophical about the whole affair:

> Our programme was delayed by a crucial week by the technicians' strike, and the BBC pipped us to the post by two days. There are those here at Thames who feel that we deserved the plaudits and they did not. I think that's entirely wrong in the sense that a news programme with two major bulletins each evening to play with can get a bandwagon rolling in a way that a single documentary can never do. Witness *Seeds of Despair*, which got a good deal of response, but certainly didn't get a bandwagon rolling when one might have rolled in July.

> One of the effects of our technicians' dispute was that we got our documentary out, but we were not allowed to give any to ITN. They were absolutely screaming because that was during the absolutely crucial period when ITN were being beaten, and very badly beaten, by the BBC.

> *Bitter Harvest*, in association with the BBC's news coverage did contribute to getting the Ethiopian famine recognised as a major issue. The fact that there were two days of hard-news coverage on the BBC, which was quite rightly stressing the suffering, and simply the suffering, in northern Ethiopia, followed by our coming in on the Thursday night with half an hour of the essential politics before an audience of 6 to 7 million contributed what was precisely the right combination of news and current affairs and with precisely the right timing. This is why I don't go along with my colleagues who say we should have been picking up the plaudits, because frankly there wouldn't have been any.

Why did this particular bandwagon roll? What was so special about the Amin-Buerk film? One of the essential truths about journalism is that really big stories like this cannot be predicted in advance – there is almost always an unforeseen series of factors which combine to magnify the impact. In the case of Ethiopia '84 there were several.

First, the Ethiopian authorities were keeping journalists out of the famine areas throughout August and September. Thus, when the rains failed and the journalists returned in October, conditions had deteriorated very rapidly, people were dying in huge numbers, millions were under threat of death, and the images and sounds were therefore far more dramatic than in July. The accidental and last-minute pairing of Amin and Buerk was also important. A different cameraman, a different correspondent and the film might have died forgotten, like so many others. Had the story broken a year later, when South Africa had become a hotter news story, it's unlikely that Buerk could have been spared to go to Ethiopia.

It was also a relatively flat time for news in Europe – there were no great stories already commanding the headlines at that time. Had there been, say, a war in the Middle East, Amin's film might well have struggled to attract attention. Then there was the coincidence of record grain harvests in Britain in particular, and in western Europe in general. Images of Norfolk farmers wading through grain mountains sat uneasily in people's minds with images of death from starvation in Korem and Makelle. The public in the west had also now become slightly more conscious of the politics of famine; in 1973 everyone was inclined to regard famine as an act of God and to blame it on the weather; but by 1984 perceptions were sharpening.

The biblical image too which Buerk has mentioned, and which also struck Peter Gill, may well have played an important role at the psychological level. Here were people in long, flowing robes looking very much like familiar figures from long-forgotten Bibles. The evident dignity with which they endured their suffering also touched chords in the soft, self-indulgent west. In particular, the image of the wall at Makelle left a deep impression. On the one side about 150 people, randomly selected, lined up to collect food. On the other side of the four-foot wall there was no food for something like 10,000 people. They were starving to death. But nobody tried to cross the wall. They watched calmly and without showing resentment. That made many of us in the west uncomfortably aware that in the same circumstances we might not have behaved like that.

Chris Cramer is also quite convinced – though he is in a minority – that ENG played an important role, because this was the first time the west had witnessed the full horror of famine on tape, as opposed to 16mm film: 'Tape is just a better picture. Film tends to be still a bit scratchy and lacking in depth, and ENG is for real'. Gill's documentary, however, was on film; union rules forbid the use of ENG on *TV Eye* or *World in Action*.

But over and above all these considerations perhaps was the way in which the BBC handled the film. For a start, by leading on two consecutive days with items of eight and seven minutes in length – in a news programme where two minutes was the norm – the BBC was quite clearly saying: 'Here is an event of major importance' and this obviously helped to maximise its impact. Secondly, the BBC alone as an institution has the power and ability, with all the outlets it commands, to make a story run and run, once it is sure, as in this case, of overwhelming popular interest. So the story was retold and kept running on BBC TV, on the regional television stations, and on home, local and World Service radio. No independent television company and no newspaper could have acted in quite this way. It also made eminent commercial sense for the BBC, in its rivalry with ITV, to stay with the story, which it presented, misleadingly, as its own 'exclusive'. So a combination of public opinion, the institutional structure of the BBC and commercial rivalry all combined to keep the Ethiopian famine in the news.

Neither Amin nor Buerk had any inkling of the impact their film was to make. But then how could they? Amin recalls that:

> Obviously, I felt that this was going to move a lot of people and that there would be a lot of help but, as has happened on several stories before, I thought that it would be forgotten quickly. But the world stayed with this story and the help that was given by ordinary people around the world helped to save millions of lives in Ethiopia and in other parts of Africa.

> I think the special thing on this particular story was the fact that you could point a camera in any direction and see children, mothers, fathers, dying in front of you. I think the scale of the disaster was such that it had to hit the conscience of anybody who was looking at it. Just about everyone who sees these pictures – and I have seen hundreds looking at them – breaks down and cries. So it was just an unbelievable situation in a time when we take so much for granted, particularly food.

Michael Buerk had a similar reaction:

> I didn't think that anybody who was not there could share much more than a small proportion of the feelings by experiencing it at third hand, sitting in the comfort of their own living rooms.

Photographers and journalists spring into action as the paths of Bob Geldof and Mother Teresa cross in the airport lounge at Addis Ababa.

I didn't think that it could translate itself to somebody in a different circumstance in quite the same way. I felt the thing would have an impact, that it would move people. But I didn't imagine that it would move them in quite the way it did or quite as extensively as it did.

One tends to underestimate the intelligence of the viewing audience; certainly, I think, to underestimate the nobility of people's sentiments – if that isn't too pompous a phrase. People are moved by other people's distress if it's sufficiently out of the ordinary. People's sensitivity becomes dulled by repetition perhaps.

Everything about the British and other publics proved to be wrong. I remember talking to NBC, who also ran the piece and had this amazing reaction. They told me: 'It'll only last a week; the American public will soon get bored with that sort of stuff.' I almost agreed with them at the time, but they proved to be terribly wrong.

Buerk soon found himself under considerable pressure to return to Ethiopia, but:

I was reluctant to get involved in what I considered to be spurious news stories about shipments of whisky going to

Ethiopia while other people were starving, because I felt this wasn't really that important. I didn't want to get in the way of the overall truthful reporting of Ethiopia; on the other hand I didn't want to go and do something that wasn't really relevant that might inhibit the flow of aid. It would be silly not to say that I wasn't terribly proud of the reaction the films had caused. I did a lot of things privately, and just a couple of things publicly, but I didn't want to be doing a Geldof – I was really glad that Geldof was being Geldof.

Perhaps more than any other reason for the continuing impact of the films was their effect on Bob Geldof, then known only as lead singer of the Boomtown Rats. The films had moved him not just to compassion but to action. Within days he had formed Band Aid and organised a recording with stars like Sting, Spandau Ballet and Phil Collins. The song they made, *Do They Know It's Christmas?* went on to become the biggest-selling record of all time.

It was followed by Live Aid, the 'global juke box', which took place simultaneously in London and Philadelphia in July 1985, broke new ground in worldwide satellite communications and had raised over $100 million by mid-1986.

Geldof's use of the media was a lesson to everyone. His tactless charm and direct style gave him an appeal to public and press alike. In January 1985 he went to Ethiopia, together with a plane-load of journalists. The contrast between his media circus and Buerk's visit some weeks earlier was striking.

When Geldof arrived in Ethiopia for the first time, doors opened. With the gaze of the world upon it, and perhaps thinking of the revolution brought on by hiding the '73 famine, the Ethiopian government laid on all the facilities it could muster. It even arranged special flights to areas where 'security' was a problem. By coincidence Mother Teresa was leaving Addis for Calcutta the same day, and Geldof wanted to meet her. Paul Harrison was at the airport when Geldof flew in:

> It was as if the Yugoslavian nun and the Irish pop singer were working together to push the Ethiopian authorities. She was telling Bob of the palaces she had seen, one of which was occupied by Chairman Mengistu. 'They'd make fine orphan-ages.' she said. The Ethiopians started looking uncomfortable.

Michael Buerk (left) and Mohamed Amin (centre) receiving the Royal
Television Society award for the best international news story of 1984.
Sir Huw Wheldon, then President of the Society, presented the award
at the Dorchester Hotel on 21 February 1985.

One of them stood in front of my camera. Another indicated to
me to switch off. 'The interview is over'.

But it continued regardless, in front of the world's press. It was
the day before the Ethiopian Christmas and Geldof wanted to go
to Lalibela, the heart of Ethiopian Christianity. Few of the foreign

community had been allowed there as it was the centre of a lot of fighting. Amazingly, though, Geldof got his way. The trip, in an ancient Dakota, was broken at Kombolcha, a Russian military airfield:

> We all got out and stretched our legs while the bigwigs tried to contact Lalibela by radio. They couldn't get any reply. So we took off anyway! We landed at Lalibela at dusk and were hustled out of the plane down a ricketty stepladder. The door slammed shut behind us. The pilot was so worried about a rebel attack that he nearly took off with two of the BBC's boxes of equipment.
>
> We were taken to a hotel where some soldiers were billeted. They were all turned out. We slept in their rooms under Red Cross blankets, while they slept in their clothes on the dirt outside. It was Christmas Eve.

Geldof went on to tour the refugee camps. But one thing he refused to do was to be photographed with a starving child. It was the media he wanted to exploit, not the victims of famine.

Michael Buerk's part in the story was over. Within a few days of getting to London on 23 October, he had returned to his Johannesburg base:

> South Africa is the one country in the world that really couldn't care less about what's happening in Ethiopia! It was the only country that didn't show Live Aid. So I completely escaped all that furore. When they did show our Ethiopian films, about two weeks later, they'd been edited and interpolations had been put in them to indicate fairly forcefully to the audience that this famine was a result not only of a black government, but of a Marxist, military, black government, in a way that made me a little bit angry.

Buerk did return to Ethiopia again, a few weeks after the first films and then again one year later. He recollects that:

> When I went back a couple of weeks later and suddenly found these previously deserted airstrips with Hercules aircraft, and the RAF flying in, it was impossible not to be lulled into a lump

in the throat sort of 'good gracious me, if I snuff it tomorrow, at least there's one thing that I was involved in that really made a difference to somebody somewhere'.

A year later, I felt terribly hopeful about some of it, but there were signs in the film that we did at the time – 1985 – that the improvement had only been temporary, allied as it was to a greater rainfall and an ability at least in part to produce a small harvest. I came away a year after with two overriding impressions: first, how much can be done when human sympathies are engaged in that manner; but second, how little difference it actually seems to make over any long timespan. People are still scrabbling around in two-year-old seeds and dying after all that money, all that interest, and all that focus on that one particular country.

You could see the thing slipping. In two or three years' time – or perhaps it needs a cycle of ten years – somebody may go out and do exactly what Jonathan Dimbleby did in 1973 and we did in 1984. I've got that awful feeling that somebody else will be doing exactly the same in 1994, and maybe a lot earlier.

11 | News Aid?

News out of Africa has focused on the way in which three particular African famines have become stories in the western media. Each story has been distinctive. In Biafra a rugged freelance individualist, Frederick Forsyth, was involved; in Ethiopia in 1973 it was an individual, Jonathan Dimbleby, working for a company; whilst in Ethiopia in 1984 it was the companies themselves, Visnews and the BBC.

There have, however, been many common threads running through all – notably the accidental, fortuitous way in which the stories have been covered and presented. One thinks of Michael Leapman's plane not arriving to take him out of Biafra; of Jonathan Dimbleby's Sri Lankan friend happening to see his film about the Sahel and so passing on rumours of a tragedy in Ethiopia; and of Peter Gill's film being 'blacked' by the unions, thus opening the door for the reports by Mohamed Amin and Michael Buerk; and, indeed, of the unplanned and last-minute pairing of Amin and Buerk themselves.

Another thread has been the role played by determined and strong-willed individuals. In a world in which it is easy for individuals to feel themselves powerless, it is instructive and inspiring to see what can be done by people like Frs Mike and Kevin Doheny, and by Frederick Forsyth and Jonathan Dimbleby, all of whom have in different ways exploited the potential of the media.

A further striking example is, of course, Bob Geldof, a product, though a very different product, of the same Dublin school as the Dohenys. For a year and a half, this Irish pop star, with brilliant and original insight into the possibilities of the media and of satellite technology, organised a series of happenings which gave expression to the idealism of the young, which appealed to people everywhere regardless of age, sex, class or race, and which put ponderous

135

politicians the world over on the spot.

His frankness of style was all the more engaging because it contrasted so sharply with the normal discourse of politics, of journalism and of aid and development. Impatient with existing structures, Geldof created his own. Cynics were quick to claim that he was in it only for the publicity or the money. In his autobiography *Is that it?* (1986), Geldof candidly admits that his rock star status was on the wane, but he does not mention that some years earlier when the Boomtown Rats were at their peak, he had offered to raise money for a relief agency and been rebuffed. In May 1986, following the success of Sport Aid, another global event, Geldof announced that he was retiring with 'compassion fatigue'. In June 1986, he received an honorary knighthood. What lasting impact has he made?

'Geldof is a wonderful Pied Piper' argues Jonathan Dimbleby, stressing his role in attracting the young. But it should not be forgotten that by the time Geldof appeared on the scene, the ground was already better prepared. Jonathan Dimbleby believes that:

> People came to this crisis with a slightly greater level of understanding of the issues. Much more frequently you would hear people saying: 'What about development? How do you prevent this happening?' People understood that there was a distinction between emergency relief and rehabilitation and development.

> Throughout the 1970s, the schoolchildren were educated much more about these things, and they're the young adults of today. They're Geldof's generation.

Lloyd Timberlake of Earthscan agrees:

> I think there is a difference between this drought and the Sahel drought of the early '70s. Then everyone said: 'Drought – act of God, natural disaster'. But this time around there is a more heightened public awareness. People know that it's not just the weather.

> Look at the process that Oxfam's gone through. It started off saying: 'Famine – send food'. Then it said: 'No, wait a minute, famines seem to be about bad development, so we've got to get involved in development, helping villages to be less vulnerable'. Then it was: 'No, hold on a minute, we can't make the villages

less vulnerable because of the whole national and international political situation'. So suddenly quiet little Oxfam was mounting a huge march on Parliament to change all that, and getting itself into a situation where it ran up against the Charity Commission. And I think the public are following that same line of awareness, but more slowly.

It is greatly to Geldof's credit that he has recognised and emphasised the politics and made more westerners than ever before aware of the umbilical cord that binds the Third World to the west. For the west did not 'discover' the Third World – it created it, and is historically responsible for the present unequal division of wealth and resources in the world. In stressing this, Geldof has given leverage to those in the media, especially documentary film makers like Jonathan Dimbleby, Mohamed Amin and Peter Gill, who want to explore the complex links between famine in parts of Africa and plenty in parts of the west. Gill has no doubt that:

> British television, while alerting people to the African tragedy, while helping to expose it and being responsible for great public generosity, has not done anywhere near enough to peck away at the complexities of the Third World-developed world relationship. And here actually is an area where there are tremendously strong and interesting stories that someone ought to be covering.

Jonathan Dimbleby agrees that now:

> The whole question of poverty has been lifted into a debate from which it had been excluded. That's at the serious level. But at the level of popular journalism, it is still uncertain how much will and energy there is to pursue these questions.

Just as Jonathan Dimbleby's post-1973 films, and their recycling – for example, through children's television – helped inform and in a sense prepare people for the 1984 famine in Ethiopia, so the programmes and series since then, like Ali Mazrui's *The Africans*, a nine-part series shown at prime time on BBC 1 in the summer of 1986, may be having a comparable impact.

It would be naïve however to suggest that the creation of growing awareness is either a simple or an inevitable process. Just as the momentum which followed 1973 was lost, there is a possibility that the same may happen again. Although the charters of both the BBC and the Independent Broadcasting Authority stipulate that some current affairs programmes must be shown at prime time, there is a strong tendency to relegate development-type programmes to the late, late hours, or to BBC 2 or Channel 4, or to both. Moreover, television producers, in Peter Gill's experience, have an inbuilt resistance to programmes about the Third World:

> There is a weary and unjustified cynicism about public interest in this issue that is widespread within the media. I think a lot of television producers underestimate the genuine public concern and interest in this area.

It is true that commercial rivalries may have helped to 'sell' the 1984 famine in Ethiopia. As Lloyd Timberlake asserts:

> There's got to be a profit in the story before the media, which really draws attention to things, gets hooked into it. Because the media are really a bunch of competing private guys, it's always haphazard.

But competition is no reason for complacency. If commercial considerations had loomed large in the minds of those at the BBC who decided to 'push' the story, they could equally have conspired to kill it. As Jonathan Dimbleby suggests, the fact that the Amin-Buerk film 'arose out of a series of accidents is a demonstration that one must remain sceptical about any news organisation's compassion or feeling'.

Similarly, despite Peter Gill's role in reporting the 1984 Ethiopian famine, his employers, Thames Television, were singularly unenthusiastic when he wanted to follow this up by writing a book about the response of the various agencies to that famine. It will be interesting to see whether Gill will ever be able to realise one of his major ambitions. This is to make a famine story without a single starving child in sight; to concentrate on what he believes to be the equally dramatic side of famine prevention and preparation, and to do so without employing the sterile cliché of the white 'Angel of Mercy' and by stressing, by contrast, the positive role of African agencies like the Ethiopian RRC. As Rob Stephenson of the Relief and Development Institute says:

> I would like more understanding on the part of the public of the reality of what's going on inside agencies, inside the UN and inside a relief operation. Somehow the reality never comes

across. And I think there's always this feeling that if one presents it as it really is, in its messiness, in its cultural confusion, the public will switch off and not give money. That barrier can be changed. You can say look, this is actually an amazingly interesting, complex and difficult job.

There remains the danger, stressed by UN's Djibril Diallo – one perhaps impossible to overcome in the present direction of media trends of faster and faster news – of the 'quick and headline-seeking superficial coverage', which seizes on the dramatic and the exceptional, but fails to place it in any meaningful context. The demise of the foreign correspondent, notably in newspapers and television, has reinforced this trend. Despite this, Diallo says:

> We must build on the evidence that enough hard-bitten media professionals and their hard-bitten 'gatekeepers' back home have themselves understood that they have an important but extraordinarily delicate and sensitive role in building bridges of real understanding between the millions who have responded with such compassion, and the millions of Africans who have never lost their pride and dignity even in the deepest destitution.

The new technology, with satellites now in routine use and with 'World Service' television just around the corner, whilst apparently opening doors to greater mutual comprehension, is no guarantor of this. As Oscar Wilde is reputed to have said, when asked whether the opening of telephone links between Europe and America would be a good thing: 'It all depends on whether you have anything to say.' Stewart Purvis of *Channel 4 News* comments on current technology in similar vein:

> The technology nowadays allows us to do anything we want, if we have a mind to do it. We could transmit live from Tristan da Cunha, in the middle of the South Atlantic. Technology is not a bar, given the will.

> We've just about got past the stage of 'today's pictures' for their own sake. Now we are beginning to ask ourselves what we can do with the new technology. More and more material will be available sooner and faster. It will be an engineering extravaganza, but the right decisions about what to do with it all will have to be made by the people back at base.

Select Bibliography

Books

Peter Cutler and Robin Stephenson. *The State of Food Emergency Preparedness in Ethiopia* (1984) Relief and Development Institute, formerly International Disaster Institute, London.

Djibril Diallo. *African Reflections on a Famine* (1985) International Symposium on Drought and Desertification, Washington, D.C.

Frederick Forsyth. *The Biafra Story* (1969) Penguin, London. (1983) Severn House, London, with new Foreword and Afterword.

Bob Geldof. *Is that it?* (1986) Sidgwick and Jackson, London.

Peter Gill. *A Year in the Death of Africa* (1986) Paladin, London.

Graham Hancock. *Ethiopia: The Challenge of Hunger* (1985) Victor Gollancz, London.

Preston King. *An African Winter* (1986) Penguin, London.

Liam Nolan. *The Forgotten Famine* (1974) Mercier Press, Dublin.

The Relief and Rehabilitation Commission. *The Challenges of Drought* (1985) RRC, Addis Ababa.

Jack Shepherd. *The Politics of Starvation* (1975) Carnegie Endowment for International Peace, New York and Washington, D.C.

Lloyd Timberlake. *Africa in Crisis* (1985) Earthscan, London.

Articles

Jonathan Dimbleby. 'The hidden hunger', *The Guardian*, 18 October 1973.

Jonathan Dimbleby. 'Faint hope and charity', *The Guardian*, 20 March 1974.

John Durniak. 'The Pulitzer puzzle', *Popular Photography*, October 1984, 64-5, 86-8.

Arshad Gamiet. 'Mohamed Amin: a life in pictures', *Arabia*, June 1985, 87-91.

Tony Hall. 'Keeping out news', *Africa Emergency Report*, No.4, September-October 1985, 5.

John Isaac, Anthony Suau and Stan Grossfield. 'On location', *American Photographer*, May 1985, 98-100.

Colin Legum. 'The night they 'hanged' Selassie', *The Observer*, 15 September 1974.

Hailu Lemma. 'The politics of famine in Ethiopia', *Review of African Political Economy*, No.33, 1985, 44-58.

David Markus. 'Moving pictures', *American Photographer*, May 1985, 50-53.

Index

144   Index

also from **Hilary Shipman**

by

ALICE COLEMAN

'UTOPIA ON TRIAL should be prescribed reading for every planner, architect, MP and councillor concerned with housing in Britain'

Christopher Booker, Daily Mail

'. . . should have as profound an effect on town planners as did Jane Jacobs' classic *The Death and Life of Great American Cities*'

Keith Waterhouse, The Mirror

'It is perhaps the most scathing critique yet of the squalor and social breakdown produced by the utopian visions that built many huge council estates'

Deyan Sudjic, The Sunday Times